T0365648

The
Black
Book

The Black Book

Mr. John

PARTRIDGE

To order additional copies of this book, contact
Toll Free 800 101 2657 (Singapore)
Toll Free 1 800 81 7340 (Malaysia)
orders.singapore@partridgepublishing.com

www.partridgepublishing.com/singapore

INTRODUCTION

A Book with a Difference – or Maybe Not

This book is a little different from the ones I've written before. It is a book of moments and direct snapshots of my thoughts. This is why I called it "The Black Book", as I write my thoughts, opinion and express my feeling without worry of being politically correct, it a book of thoughts, some light, dark and other black. There are also drawings and words, quickly scribbled down in the spur of the moment. They may not seem to make any sense at first glance, but don't worry. I'll help to interpret them for you, and if you keep an open mind, we might be able to share something meaningful.

As with my other books, this one will be sort of a journey, so I hope you'll enjoy it. And before I forget, I'd like to thank all the people who have entertained me over the past fifty-eight years. My gratitude to those I have met, and those I have not met, and those I would never want to meet.

NEW YEAR'S EVE

If you are young and you drink a great deal it will spoil your health, slow your mind, make you fat – in other words, turn you into an adult.

—P. J. O'Rourke

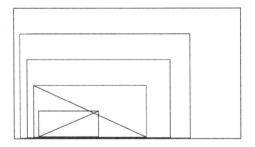

Tick! Tick! Loud music. Tick! Tick! Frantic dance moves. Tick! Tick! Alcohol is being consumed at an alarming rate. Tick! Tick! There is heat, sweat, smiles, laughter, and even cries, but still no blood on the dance floor (thank goodness). Tick! Tick! Ten, nine, eight, seven, six, five, four, three, two, one, Happy New Year! For a moment, you might think you're in heaven, but you're really living in hell. It sounds terrible and overly dramatic, I know, but what I'm trying to say is you should stop living a lie and live the truth. Still dramatic, I know.

But before you question my penchant for drama, ask yourself this: do I live my own life, or do I live the life others want or expect me to live?

I'll get back to that question in good time, I promise. Right now, I'm drifting away into my own head and letting the voices within talk to me. They speak, and then it occurs to me. For children, the world can be a wondrous place. They take the time to explore and get absorbed in all that is around them. Let me ask you this: How many minutes does it take an adult to travel twenty metres, compared to a toddler? I'm not referring to our ability to walk faster; I'm referring to our inability to see and explore every step we take. Do we, as adults, really see the world, or do we move through each day in a state of semiconsciousness? Are we like a ball in a pinball machine, being flicked and pushed, bouncing from point to point? Do we only stop or come to rest when our fingers, eyes, and brains lose the ability to redirect the silver ball? Do we just let it slam into the holding zone until it gets flicked again? Will our journey – or should I say *game* – be able to start again?

Music allows us to explore our feelings. We escape through the melodies and lyrics of a songwriter, who escaped through his or her ability to share words and emotions through song. Happy New Year, everybody.

Music is a moral law. It gives soul to the universe, wings to the mind, flight to the imagination, and charm and gaiety to life and to everything.

—Plato

It's the second of January, which is my first day back at work. Shouts of 'Happy New Year!' echo throughout the building, with smiles and handshakes. It sounds like the majority of people are happy to see another year pass by and announce, with passion, the beginning of a new phase in their lives. But what has changed, apart from the fact we went to bed (if we did go to bed) and a few seconds, minutes, and hours passed by? We can now say that we are a year older, or a little older at the least. We still have the same lives, albeit in a different phase of the human calendar. The only thing that has truly changed is the digit that represents the number of years that have passed since man first started to record and register the passing of time. Another year has gone, and a new year has come, but still we live on – tick, tick, tick.

Now it is the fifth of January. You may run, swim, or fly, but still, the clock of life continues to tick away. By now people have moved from wishing each other 'Happy New Year' to saying, 'Good morning', 'Good evening', and 'Good night' again, as the excitement of the beginning of this New Year has disappeared. People are now getting back to their day-to-day routines. January goes by, and the other months pass with ease. Soon people are thinking about another party and celebrating the end of another year. Tick, tick, tick. Not many give much thought to the fact that each year that goes takes us closer to that final celebration, which we shall all attend without fail. After all, there is never a failure or any discrimination when the clock stops tick-tick-ticking and we take our last breaths.

Tick, tick, tick – and the light goes on. A smile appears on my face as I rush to the airport to say 'G'day!' to my son, Liam, as he arrives from Australia on 6 January 2013. It is truly a lucky day. Thank you, God, for giving me this day and all the days since my children were born. I am truly a lucky man to have had two wonderful gifts, Claire and Liam. Love you both.

Keep the music playing and stay happy. As long as the seconds, minutes, and hours keep coming – tick, tick, tick – life is good. We exchange hugs and small talk, and now we go off to bed. Another day has gone, but what a beautiful and satisfying one it has been.

I left work at the normal time, but tonight I shall meet Liam for a beer. I had a couple of beers, and the alcohol went straight to my head. So we went home and ate dinner. Being slightly drunk and full, I kind of lost my mind. Thoughts of reality, chaos, and brilliance appeared. The first thing that rushed and crashed into my mind, which spurred my fingers to type, was 'Too much order disables the ability to be creative. Brilliance is not dreamt; it is lived.' After dreaming and waking up, you may realise that you were not asleep; you were just resting your outer casing whilst the true inner you is alive and exploring the unexplored.

I turn the music up. The sound I wish for is Eric Burdon declaring, 'War!', which allows me to play some hidden melodies from my small and well-used Hohner harmonica. It has awakened me to the sounds of harmony, and even if I don't know how to play, I'm playing it anyway. This allows me to escape to another land where my ears listen to the people within my head. Whilst creating new sounds with my own music, I am being alive and living. Tick, tick, tick – good night, everybody.

One good thing about music, when it hits you, you feel no pain.

—**Bob Marley**

I have a meeting tomorrow where I have to be all corporate and impressive, reciting figures and statistics that drown away any original thoughts about existence. Day to day, routines take away time – tick, tick, tick – while we earn a living. But still, it's important to enjoy life as it's meant to be enjoyed, even if it means you have to be a little normal.

Another month has gone, and this year is passing quickly. I've already heard people talking about next year. This was no slip of the tongue; they meant the New Year. Some people are actually wishing for another eleven months to disappear soon, so they can celebrate the ending of another year – tick, tick, tick. If I had a magic stopwatch, I would stop time, not to live in the past or to stop the future from coming but to allow myself to enjoy the current moment. I'm listening to the words within a great blues number, 'I'd Rather Be Blind than See You Go,' by Lean Russel. I would not wish to be blind, but it's hard to watch things leave me, like a beautiful day with my children, friends, or family. To wish that another day would pass, just because today was hard, is an utter waste of a wish and of time.

Good morning! I've got one of my cloudy heads today. Maybe it's thanks to the last glass of wine I had, or was it the last bottle? Or was it the last three bottles before that last one tippled down my throat? Thankfully I still managed to have my morning swim and communicate in a semi-logical way. Now I've eaten my breakfast and drunk coffee that's blacker than black, so my brain is now starting to become aware of the noise and the beauty around me. Should this chapter come with a health warning? No, maybe it should come with a notice instead, saying, 'Hello! This is the third book by a person who likes to write without malaise and even sometimes without thinking. After all, it's great to just write and then read and think, *who wrote that shit?*'

What is clear is that we cannot have inner peace without warmth and a harmonious outer world. The outer world is created by others, and we are just a speck within billions and trillions of specks. Maybe we are not the most perfect of beings, which is an accurate way of describing mankind, but – and there is always a *but* – this world is a beautiful place, and the universe we share is beyond my scope of imagination. What I can see, feel, and say is that life is about understanding that we are all individuals – different but the same.

'Bullshit!' I may hear a reader saying, thinking of the some who have everything and others who have nothing, apart from their dying breath. That is the equaliser, understanding we are different but equal, not in what we own but as people of this world. We are equal, we all bleed, we all feel pain, and we all die. As a good friend, my best friend of mine, "my wife" who is Buddhist, said when we were talking about the prediction of the end of the world, 'I shall laugh and hold the hands of the person I love.'

'Laugh?' I asked.

'Yes,' she said. She explained that she'll be happy, being with the person she loves. As they close their eyes, she shall know that rich, poor, strong, or weak, all living creatures shall be equal. There will be no discrimination due to religion, colour, age, sex, and all those other things that have caused wars and envy.

Time may continue to tick, but that big countdown has long passed, and the New Year's party headache is cleared. The year is now in full swing. The chameleon within us all makes us change to suit our environment. All the goodwill that was expressed as the clock struck twelve, and within the first few days of the New Year, is now lost. We're now busy rushing and striving to get through each day, the here and now of our lives.

Write it on your heart that every day is the best day in the year.

—**Ralph Waldo Emerson**

I think we shouldn't get too caught up with the here and now. Instead, we should come out to play. As you may have realised, the here and now parts of our lives are so filled with activity. This busy-ness stops us from dwelling on the past and even better, stops us worrying about the future. The here and now is to live for today and enjoy each and every day we have. Do this by understanding each and every thing that happens, either good or bad. Everything is an experience, and our experiences prove that we are alive.

If you surrender completely to the moments as they pass, you live more richly those moments.

—**Anne Morrow Lindbergh**

Why are we so paranoid about time? Time has become such a tightly regulated commodity, we are scared of wasting any of it. The University of Michigan stated that children today have just half as much free time as they did thirty years ago. Why? Well, because of society's and parents' fears that they won't be successful. So they enrol their kids in adult-led activities (time crunching), thinking those extra lessons will make them smarter. Peter Pan would be unhappy. 'Let them play!' I hear him shout.

Play isn't just beneficial for young minds; older ones need it too. If we do not take time for fun, we shall, in the boom and bust cycle of life, be so busy working that we start to live to work and not work to live. Dr Stephen Briers said, 'Let's not get to eighty-five to find ourselves run ragged and raw because amidst all our hectic activity, we never made time for quite enough "moments".' I would like to call these 'play moments,' which can be anything that you enjoy, even if it means being a couch potato every now and then, as long as it makes you relax, smile, and enjoy yourself. Psychologist Brian Sutton-Smith concluded grimly that 'The opposite of play is not work. It's depression.' So please take time to play, smile, and enjoy life, as it can be good.

I'm now awake, and the sun is just starting to rise. Its golden rays will send warmth into all who live underneath and maybe even burn some who try to take advantage of its strength and kindness.

My dear friend and editor Adline said, 'John you quite often go for the throat. Let's try not to be so abrupt. Let's try and ease into new topics' as I do listen and always respect her views, I am now easing into the next topic. Are you sitting comfortably and relaxed? If so, I would now like you to consider the demographics of your country's population in general. Even without knowing where you live or where you are from, I know for certain that the population of most countries is growing due to modern medicine and better healthcare, resulting in improved mortality rates. More babies survive to grow and explore, and older people are living longer, to explore some more. However, as we grow and reach certain ages, we start to look at our world differently.

In our mid-twenties and thirties, we often make a conscious effort to cast off some of our more reckless habits. We go through a phase when we try to make ourselves more sensible and responsible. That is very healthy. I was thirty-three when I realised my brain was stronger than my body. It took me another twenty-two years to totally understand myself and, more importantly, accept myself as I am. So, if you're reading this and you've left your twenties and thirties behind some decades ago, I'd like to strongly suggest that we, the young at heart but old of bones, start to loosen up a little. It is uncomfortable enough to wrestle with stiff joints; we really don't want to have stiff attitudes to accompany them. It is time now to rediscover your love for something you last did when you were much younger.

Why? You may ask All I shall say is, because you can, and you should. Even if it seems silly. What's wrong with being mature, but a little silly? I know when I laugh, I feel good. I'm sure you have heard the saying, 'laughter is the medicine of a healthy spirit and soul.'

You must always believe in yourself and always try to be your own hero. I am not asking you to wear Lycra suits, don a mask, jump tall buildings, or run faster than a speeding bullet. What I am suggesting is for you to understand your world, acknowledge all the pain and suffering that accompanies so much of life, and smile through it. This is not easy, I know, for how do we offer sunshine and roses at the end of each day? It is by putting things into perspective. Just another thought: Is it wise for us to consider the misfortunes of others, so that we can be happy with what we have and say those mystical words, 'See, it could be worse'?

You may have read in one of my previous books that life and everything within it is just a game, and how we choose to play that game will reflect on how we receive the torments, pleasures, pain, and sufferings until the end. The million-dollar question is, Why do we elect to play such games? And the answer is simple. We have limited choices. None of us asked to be born; that was the choice of our parents. Once we were born, the game was on, and we will continue to play it until we take our last breath. The majority of people elect to continue to play, rather than to stop playing, as stopping means the end, and the end means we are dead.

This will come to us all. So play hard without expecting a release, or for anything to get better. Just accept each day as another occasion to thank the game-keeper for another experience to share our torments, pleasure, pain, and sufferings with those who are in our teams. In all, there are over seven billion players, and all are striving to score that winning goal. We're all trying to get a touchdown, and we shall never truly understand all the plays or players, but one thing's guaranteed. In the end, we all finish with an equal score.

So don't let your heart become tired when you think life's game is too hard. The game you are playing is made up of rules created by others, which are removing the enjoyment and fun. This is now decision time. We can elect to continue to play by the rules of others or design a new game and play by our own rules (Please don't break the law, though!). The rules we are made to adhere to in life are often the rules – or should I say pressures and demands – of others, who want to get us to do something we don't want to do. To this, I say stop, or even fuck it, and relax. As the old saying goes, you can lead a horse to water, but you can't make it drink.

23 February 2013: Imagine waking up to a dream (or nightmare) of hardened arteries and the sound of the doctor's knife slicing through your skin. Exposed are the swollen and blocked veins that once pumped lifesaving particles of goodness within your blood. Over time, those free-flowing channels that made you grow, feel well, and stay strong became blocked. They are corroding and failing due to good and bad living habits. Your heart struggles, and the strong beat is no more than a flutter, with intermittent thumps of stress. The thickened sludge that once flowed freely is now a darkened gel compared to its former self, a vibrant, fast-moving, brilliant red liquid.

Then, when all is going south, the amazing survival commando within you sends a message to the brain to deliver an electric buzz. The shock awakens your internal pistons, pushing them to gain some inner strength with the aim of rejuvenating the dying cells and push forward, ensuring we awaken again. If we hear those inner voices, we may just be given another chance to live a little longer. Maybe then we'll clean up our act by eating better, exercising more, and drinking less. But whatever we choose to do, when the grim reaper calls you, you can't hang a 'Do not disturb' sign and think that it will go away. When it is time, it is time.

1 March 2013: I've been out all night – whoopee! What was meant to be a relaxing evening of intellectual exchange quickly turned into a long night of listening to mature men talk rubbish, thinking their stories are believable.

I've always said that I believe in Peter Pan, but tonight, even Peter Pan is more believable than listening to two bulls in a bar, measuring their horns. I went home feeling absolutely lost in my own time. All I wanted was to be able to speak English with another person and communicate in normal words, without having to break down a sentence into baby talk. I never read the *Janet and John* books that were designed for young people to learn how to read. (Well, maybe once at the red house, a special school I went to for special needs kids. What a horrible phrase.)

As I've mentioned, this book is a little different. From here, it's just going to be a book of moments and direct snapshots of my thoughts. In the first few chapters I shall add drawings and handwritten words, which were scribbled down quickly without being edited, typed, proofread, or made grammatically sound. The collection of moments I'm about to share has been produced over years, but I can say without hesitation that my drawings have not improved over time.

All people have several faces that they use to greet each and every day. The faces of a baby, father, mother, or grandparent, as well as the faces of people who are happy or sad, all portray a moment. Babies can turn from a loving, gurgling little bundle of joy to a screaming, red-faced demon in seconds. And this, on the outside, is telling us that they want something or don't want something. But as we grow older, in most cases, we don't have such tantrums (or do we?)

The difference is, young children release their tensions by blowing off steam unknowingly. This can even be very healthy. However, adults learn to control these outbursts. The faces we show doesn't always match how we feel within, where our internal pressure cooker is bubbling away, wanting to explode.

Draw and write:	

CHAPTER 2

The English Fourth Baron Raglan, Major FitzRoy Richard Somerset of the Queen's Grenadiers Guards, once remarked that 'Culture is roughly everything we do and monkeys don't.'

Why are people hot-tempered? Why can't we just learn to be calm, relaxed, and accepting? Sometimes, things, people, and situations will not be as we want, expect, or like them to be. This is life, and such are the rules of the world, universe, and, I daresay, beyond.

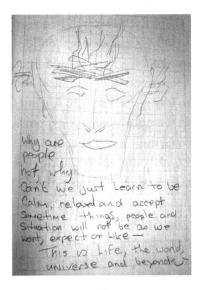

Have you ever thought about, pondered, or even questioned the meaning of existence or where we came from? How did we evolve to be who we are now? Are we all really directly descended from Adam and Eve? And if you believe this, where did Adam and Eve come from? It's not a trick question, and I'm not asking you this to test your faith or beliefs. Furthermore, I don't mean it in the Biblical sense. Rather, I'd like to discuss our roots. Honestly, how far back can we trace our roots? A few centuries? Perhaps even more, if the country we were born in kept accurate records of all births, marriages, and deaths. Many British and European countries began keeping birth, death, and marriage records at the national level back in the nineteenth century. Prior to that, these events can be found recorded in the registers of christenings, marriages, and burials maintained by parish churches.

Now, let's say, for example, that our forefathers came from a rural area, or even a forest or jungle – the middle of nowhere, basically – and let's say that they're not one of the privileged few. This means that it's unlikely that they'll find themselves a position in the history books, to be read by the masses across the centuries. Indeed, most of us came from normal folk, so unless our ancestors kept diaries and records, which would have required that they could write, generally we must rely on national and parish records, which, to be very generous, would give us a window of about five to six hundred years.

Now, let's use our imaginations and consider what things were like two hundred thousand years ago. Could I perhaps convince you that you are related to Neanderthals, or one of those groups of homo sapiens that started to leave Africa sixty to seventy thousand years ago to populate the world? Is it plausible, or even possible, that mankind, as it lives and populates the world today, cannot survive without its iPhones, BlackBerries, and other man-made luxuries? Then again, we do tend to whinge and cry about the most mundane of things.

To enlighten you and even challenge your thoughts, I will say it could it be possible that your ancestors were within the groups that destroyed the Neanderthals. Shock! Horror! But yes, I am suggesting that even thousands of years ago, we could not live in peace with others. This is well before formalised governments and religious groups were even considered.

Before I rant and rave about how this group became modern humans, I'd like to point out that over the last forty or fifty thousand years, the human species was able to survive without GPS, Facebook, and large shopping malls, the modern-day arena for open warfare due to overzealous bag-carrying and trolley-pushing pensioners – and we should not forget shopaholics and others who flock and crowd into the shops to gain comfort in the free air conditioning instead of enjoying our even freer polluted air.

Anyway, back to our ancestors. They had the power and imagination to adapt to the climate and environment until our forefathers decided to settle and call it home, thanks to their ability to hunt, fish, and survive. Or maybe their final destination was not due to any of the above. Maybe their legs were just tired, or their nagging partners said, 'Enough is enough!' or their offspring kept on asking, 'Are we there yet?'

Whatever the reason was, our ancestors had the ability to learn, improve, and, I would argue, start to believe that we were the superior species. Worse still, they thought we were in charge of the environment, and it was these actions that we can blame for the extinction of thousands of species.

Who knows? In the past our ancestors might have come close to extinction. A great book titled *Wired for Culture*, by Mark Pagel, explores this idea. I would recommend it to anyone who wonders 'what if.' I had always believed that we did not become extinct due to our ability to adapt, kill, and destroy others to survive. Therefore, I was amazed when I read the following:

> In fact, genetic studies now reveal that our ancestors might have dwindled to as few as 10,000 individuals – some say even fewer – making humans as endangered 80,000 years ago as a rhinoceros is today. Then our numbers began to grow and human

culture began to flourish, and our species, having come perilously close to extinction, reached a point of no return. Our minds were now firmly in execution control of our fates, and were showing the adaptability, and producing the artefacts and culture that would propel us out of Africa and then around the world.

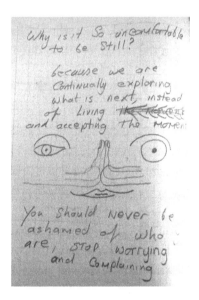

Why is it so uncomfortable for us to be still? It's because we are continually exploring what is next, instead of living and accepting the moment. You should never be ashamed of who you are, so stop worrying and complaining!

Here is another strange little drawing, with words scribbled without much thought at the given time. I was just looking for escape. Is it possible to really escape and relax considering all the things that we have now? From international travel to the Internet and mega buildings to phones, our curiosity and drive to achieve, compete, adapt, improve, and create new things never ends.

Why do we need some of those new things anyway? Most of them don't add any true value to humankind. Or do they? I think I would answer this by saying, because we have evolved, we can, and when we can, in most cases we do.

I wonder what our ancestors, who left Africa so long ago to populate distant lands, would think of us, and what we would think of them, apart from that they are uncivilised. Are we better, because of our ability to think, create, and adapt even more? Don't hurt your brain by trying to move through time to where the air was cleaner and those first human-like people were 'wild.' As time travel has not yet been developed, I shall ask that you think of the year 1900 and list the things that we have invented, found, and created in the past hundred years. Our advancements are no doubt outstanding and amazing, but is our air cleaner? And are we less wild and more civilised with all our advancements?

As humans, we are still adapting, but not to nature. Rather, we are adapting to the things that we humans have created and invented and that, in some cases, we feel we need: bigger houses, faster cars, and cooler gadgets. I could list more things that have no true value, other than to show off our wealth to others or our inability to say no. We need and want more and more, seemingly never satisfied with what we already have.

Tick, tick, tick. Time goes by, and as each year passes, my heart, soul, and mind become a little older. I would like to think that I also become a little wiser, even if my bodily functions are not as good as they used to be. Age does bring a degree of forgiveness. I am now forgiven for being politically incorrect and socially inappropriate for passing wind in a louder-than-normal fashion (and by 'normal,' I mean that squeeze-your-buttocks-together squeaking sound).

I am content with my life, my age, and those little moments that make people stare and smile, not with me but at me. Any smile, in my mind, is so much better than a frown. The words surrounding my very bad drawing of a car, ring, and lump of gold, which in my mind portrays how we humans have grown from a race that was happy to be able to survive and sleep to a species that continually wants more. Knowledge, ownership, money and materialistic bits that truly have limited value, maybe we shall kill ourselves and our plants due to our wants. Wanting has become a human disease in my opinion, one that I have suffered and may still suffer.

Wanting doesn't stop. We always want more. It's all about I and me. I don't have a magical spell to make everyone who reads this book content with what they have. But maybe if I did, I would be wrong to think I should decide what is right or wrong for others. No one has that right, and especially not me. All I wish is for the people of the world to wake up one day, look around, and appreciate what they have. Think about others who may not have what you have, or do what you do, or have received the same opportunities as you. So don't be mean or selfish. Try to be kind and open-minded, and always give where possible. Only take what is needed, and try never to waste, be it food, water, time, or even words.

Folly is a characteristic of youth:

—Brian Browne Walker

After writing the paragraph above, I looked at the silly drawings and words that I've written and selected the following, which says:

Even when you are at the front of a crowd, it doesn't mean that you see more than another person at the back.

Even sleepers are workers and collaborators in what goes on in the Universe.

—Heraclitus

Sometimes, a person at the back can see the entire picture, whereas the people at the front can only see what they want to see, not allowing their minds to be open to change. Humans have evolved and adapted. We continually become more curious, but in some ways our social grouping can restrict our ability to accept others, like a racehorse wearing blinders. These stop the horse from seeing what is to its left and right, keeping it focused only on what is ahead – or, shall I put it in another way, keeping them in the moment.

The moments can be interesting, though. As I flick through news channels and newspapers, all I see is unhappy people blaming others and each other's wrongdoings. I think accepting others is like having a good or bad bottle of wine. You can enjoy the moment, remember the name, and come back to try it again. Or else you will remember the name and never give it a second chance.

People are individuals, and you can get a bad apple in every bushel, but that does not make the others within the bushel bad. I have heard people, including myself, generalise about how we perceive people from different nations, religious groups, and even sexualities. Then we have to eat our words. Surprise, surprise! We meet someone, and through conversation, we open communication lines, debate, and listen to different views and opinions. We may then find a point upon which we can all agree. I would say, never let your bias, social beliefs, religion, or even racism stand in the way of listening to others. Do not become what I call a 'bucket head.' What's a bucket head? Well, allow me to explain.

When I am tired, hot, or bad-tempered, when my brain is on fire, I want a bucket of cold water – not to drink, but to put my head in.

However, if I did this all the time, they might lock me up. So I shower or take a long swim. Then I breathe and relax.

So, as far as I'm concerned, we shouldn't put our heads in buckets. Have you ever had a 'bucket head' moment?

What did you write, Ned? As all Australians know, Ned Kelly (1854 or 1855 – 11 November 1880) was a bucket head, or should I say, he was the Robin Hood of bucket heads. Ned was an Irish-Australian bushranger who has become an Australian folk hero. Or was he a cold-blooded killer? Anyway, in his mind, and the mind of others, he is the symbol of Irish-Australian resistance against the Australian ruling class. Whatever we may think of him, he will never know, nor will we truly know, what drove him to do what he did.

Do we know where we are going? Of course we do, as we have Google Maps and GPS systems that continually say 'recalculating.' Is our life like our GPS system, continually recalculating and trying to find the best route (or the longest shortcut, if you have one like mine)? This drawing and the words from my mind represent the yin and yang of my life, the good and bad entwined, but driving forward, as I listen to others but trust myself.

I know where to go and not go. Trust me, or better still, trust yourself. Where to start? Let's consider what I wrote earlier, about how we have evolved and what has made us different from other living species that once roamed and still roam this land. I suggested that it was because we learnt to adapt to our environment. We also looked at how we can improve on an idea through watching and then making adjustments. So we moved from those early stone tools, spears and arrows, to automotive and robotic equipment as well as weapons of mass destruction. Our curiosity is insatiable. We continually want to know more, so we invent and create new things and cures, with the aim of making our lives easier, faster, and more pleasurable. In my opinion, sometimes we ought to limit thought. Even with all the brilliant brains working on inventions and analyses, do scientists and governments truly understand the consequences of our actions, decisions, and lack of actions or decisions? So it gives me great pleasure to come up with the no-brainer statement of: 'limited thought analyses of what is next.' I was challenged by my editor, who said, 'Don't know if we can call this a no-brainer. It seems very complex to me.' So in response, I shall offer the following thought. The future is not in your thoughts, as a thought is no more than what is known and never the unknown. This is why we continue to make mistakes, and mistakes become the new super-cures, must-have gadgets, or sometimes disasters. What is next?

I do not know what you wrote, or maybe you did not allow your mind to venture into what it knows, but I write the following to offer my thoughts. I'm not talking here of the next invention or cure but of where we are located in the evolution of mankind. Will we live another forty thousand or hundred thousand years? Or will we see the sun die in another four billion years? Whoops, that's a silly thought. None of the people who will read this book will live for another four billion years. And if the words from this book survive, I wonder how they will be communicated. What I mean is, will extinction come to us as it has come to other species? Why will it come? Will it be because of our curiosity or due to one of our own inventions or cures that went wrong? Or will our small and beautiful planet earth finally say, 'Enough is enough!' I do not want to write about doom and gloom, as my cup is always half full (if not totally full), but I am scared for the future of mankind and this beautiful place I call home.

Why? It is because our inability to live together in peace, accepting that we are different but the same. Now, as I think and explore my inner thoughts, I wonder if the destroyers of the environment shall be destroyed by the environment in turn.

We never know; our planet may just respond with force. It may finally rid this beautiful planet of its greatest destroyer, humans, and all the other innocent species that have survived and in some cases become domesticated to feed our stomachs. Following this cleansing process, the earth may lay dormant, licking its wounds. Initially exhausted, it will become calm. Peace and harmony will spread across the planet as it regrows and purifies itself again. This is until nature, or a higher power, yet again allows evolution to create another living form to roam this planet, adapt, create, and hopefully not destroy.

Life is good if we learn to live it without any malice and show respect, while opening our arms and hearts to all those around us. Smile and laugh, as this is only chapter two. Hopefully, we shall travel through and explore more of the opinions of a man who once stripped and danced at a birthday party – and it was legal and a job. (Yes, I was once a strip-o-gram.) As I always say, life is meant to be lived. I can say that I have lived, and I shall continue to live more with the blessing of God, friends, and the universe. This is until I take my final bow, with a smile and no regrets. I would like to end this chapter by saying something that I once heard someone say upon hearing his phone beep, signalling the arrival of a text message. He smiled and said, 'I am receiving love.' So I would like to send you love right now.

If you really faced the world as it is, an tackled it, you would find it something infinitely greater than any philosophy, greater than any book in the world, greater than any teaching, greater than any teacher.

—**J. Krishnamurti**

CHAPTER 3

See only what one wants to see and knowing only what one wants to know

—David Skitt

I finished the last chapter by saying that I wanted to send you love. I have written about love, not because I consider myself an expert but because I feel there is no expert in love. Love is all around, but so is hatred. This chapter shall explore even more of my mind, as I sit and write, offering my view while listening to music and wondering if my perception of this world is yours. Moreover, to answer that, I shall say it is not, as perception in an individual thing. So unless you are not an individual, which we should all be, or a clone that has had its brain removed, making independent thought impossible, our perception shall be different.

What drives a person's perception? In my opinion, perception comes from experience, education, family, social grouping, and the environment, but it is not limited to just these. Your perception grows as you grow and experience new and wonderful things or even bad and horrible things. Each and every day, we learn. The worlds within our minds grow, where we develop thoughts of what we know and never of the unknown. This does not mean we cannot be creative, but our mind works with facts, and facts come from what is known and never what is unknown. Is perception real? And as we are and should be individuals, can we expect others to accept our opinions, as those opinions and thoughts are made up from our perception and those perceptions drive our behaviours? So, is it acceptable to forgive tyrant dictators who take control of a country? Their perception of right and wrong is made up of their values, and it is these values that drive their behaviour. Bear in mind that a dictator has absolute authority and is not restricted by a constitution or laws. Do these people even see and observe what is happening? Are they blinded due to madness? Or are they driven by the knowing-doing gap, where they self-justify their actions or lack of action?

Why would a parent diligently put their seatbelt on? Is it because they want to be safe, or they want to comply with the law? Perhaps it's because they do not want to get hurt or be given a fine. If any of these is so, then why would they allow the most beautiful and irreplaceable gift in their lives, their child, to roam freely in the backseat or even sit between Mum and Dad in the front of the car? We all know it is dangerous, but in their kindness or laziness, in their desire to stop the love of their lives from shouting and screaming, they we give in and do not buckle them up. This is a simple explanation of the knowing-doing gap. Does that make the child the dictator or tyrant?

As I'm writing this chapter, in the background I hear a newsreader talking about Kim Jong-un, North Korea's communist leader. Kim Jong-un is the ruler of a country that is very secretive. What is known is that they do have nuclear weapons and a large military force. Their previous leader Kim Jong-il, father of the current leader, is dead. Kim Jong-un has been named as successor.

Democracy at its worst. STOP, I know North Korea is not democracy, but what is democracy at its best or worse? I made the statement because in my mind, democracy is a political system for choosing and replacing the government through free and fair election. It involves active participation of the people as citizens, in politics and in civic life. It also means a high standard of human rights, where all citizens are protected by rule of law and in which the laws and procedures apply equally to all citizens. From what I've read and understood about North Korea, it would appear that it is not a country where free and fair elections take place. The level of human rights granted to the citizens of North Korea is also debatable.

But what I say about North Korea may be totally incorrect, as North Korea is one of the world's most secretive states. Some information about the country and its people is known, though most is based on speculation from outside agencies. I am convinced that the government of North Korea's propaganda division is painting a totally different picture of the outside world. Some of the North Korean people may even believe what is being said is the truth. In general, people are gullible, believing what they are told, just as a child believes that his or her parents always tell the truth. With this in mind, I can only assume that Kim Jong-un was born as a normal child. He was then brought up in what he may have thought was a normal way. He never saw the wrongs but only saw what he was told there was to see. This was what he was given. He was conditioned from his very first day on Earth. It could even be argued that although he was educated outside of North Korea, his ability to accept anything else would be against the family values that were placed upon him from birth. But do parents always tell the truth?

To escape or try to change, would take this unknown but known young communist leader to new levels of unknowns. So, his choice is to live by only seeing and doing as his father did and living his father's life as well as his own life. He continues to be guided, led, and maybe even instructed by the true powers within North Korea – the generals of the armed forces that supported his father and family. To rebel, or try to enforce change, may strip him of his leadership and the power that he portrays on propaganda news, released to the rest of the world. Do we honestly believe that the people who now stand next to him would allow this young unknown to open the doors to this secretive country, so that the past fifty-plus years could be scrutinised by the West and put on display? Would the rest of the world open their hearts and minds, or would their selfishness and single-mindedness block any attempt for the North Koreans to tell their side of the story? Alternatively, would these articles be lost on the cutting room floor? As the controllers of what we read, that would include large organisation, financial analyses, economic assassins or governments, I am sure it is much easier for us to believe and sadly accept that all the trade and financial embargoes being placed on North Korea is good. However, is it really about improving the condition of the millions of North Korean people or more about taking control of another nation and forcing Western ways on a non-Western country?

Still, the power brokers and think tanks of the Western world try to dictate terms through restrictions on trade and finance. Is this really helping the North Korean people who we believe are suffering? Are these people the same people that I recently saw on TV, celebrating and chanting praises to their government? I may sound cynical, but considering all the trouble spots where millions of people's lives are being destroyed in the name of gaining democracy, maybe the world's leaders need to rethink things.

As it appears to me, sometimes the people whom we are trying to free would have more freedom if we just left them alone. I do not condone any type of violence, and I do believe that we all have the right for independence, freedom, and happiness. But – and as I always say, there is always a *but* – at what cost? One person's freedom could be another person's hell, and one person's independence could be another's death sentence. So what is happiness? How can the West, East, North, or South, or any major power, offer happiness to another country that is different culturally and religiously? People believe in different things, hold different values, and see the world differently.

No one enjoys pain and suffering. Well, then again, there are a few who do. But mankind is the only species that I know that continually inflicts pain and suffering on each other with limited consideration for the consequences and the damage that we are causing. This is the unknown ... or is it? Many may be saying, 'The unknown what?' Well, I will say it is the unknown of knowing, closing our minds so that we can act shocked and say we did not know. History books are filled with stories of the pain and suffering of war, the atrocities of years past, and the suppression of freedom. Therefore, to say this is unknown would be incorrect. It is known, but still we continually inflict pain on each other, due to differences of opinion, beliefs, and culture. The majority of the people of the world know and understand that we are different. I would even say the majority of people across the world would like to live in peace. But still governments take those people to war.

> What are your thoughts? Do we know what drives our governments?
>
>
>
>
>

The question I often think about is, do governments truly care about the people of other countries? Worse still, should they become a little more selfish and look inwards to ensure that their own people are not suffering before they try to fix the problems of others? Could America, for example, say that they do not have poverty? Could the United Kingdom say they do not have homeless people? Could Germany say they do not have racism? I could list more and more examples, but let's get back to North Korea. Will the pressures of the West, and all the restrictions being placed on the North Korean government through embargoes, limiting or freezing financial support, and other restrictions actually help the people we have been told are suffering? The answer is no. In fact, I think this would make their suffering even worse, thus allowing the North Korean government to gain even greater support from the people. However, this is just my opinion, and who am I? Well, I, John Robert Christian, a citizen of this world. What I write is my perception, which I gained from my experiences, which I call my free educational period. Schools only taught us the basics, while life teaches us the truth if we are willing and open-minded enough to allow all that we see, hear, smell, and touch to become a part of our knowledge without discrimination.

This is your last photograph, what will people see?

—JRC. Mr John

'A Boy may say: My future, my life, I need education.' A girl may say: 'If we are educated we can help others.' This is a statement, which I would say it is not an original thought as there is more than enough evidence other than the African Proverb below to indicate the differences between how the world is gender imbalanced. I will even say that large area of the world is discriminate towards girls and women, and this is a fact as they are not treated equally across this planet.

African Proverb: 'Educate a boy and you educate an individual. Educate a girl and you're educating the entire village.'

Education must be for all men, women, girls, and boys, with no segregation.

We started this chapter looking at perception, and we explored how we build on our perception. I mentioned above that in my opinion, education is not just the material we learn while at school, as we should be learning every day. While we are allowed to live on the earth, we should never restrict what a person is exposed to. I am not saying that I want a world without censorship, but I am saying we should all be allowed to explore different customs, cultures, beliefs, and values without being discriminant. This is being educated.

No one is born hating another person because of the colour of his skin, or his background, or his religion. People must learn to hate, and if they can learn to hate, they can be taught to love, for love comes more naturally to the human heart than its opposite.

—Nelson Mandela

Once the world's population is truly educated, maybe (and this is a big maybe) people will see the world not only as it appears to them, but as it appears to others. It will give us the ability to better understand and not be fooled, charmed, or emotionally sucked in. Collectively, we fear individualism, where we may be seen as different from the norm or the crowd. Our individualism could be considered unfaithful to the crowd or against popular belief, when all we are doing is doubting and questioning another view or opinion. If this is true, I have been unfaithful. I like being a sheep (follower) when the leader is a leader, but when the leader is not a leader, I shall always be an individualist and strive for change.

Across centuries, we have labelled a few people as prophets and saints and even more as great leaders. This is even though some of those leaders were also considered dictators. Sometimes, we go even further and consider elevating a few gifted people for their commitment, passion, energy, and longevity as 'world teachers'. Nevertheless, these are merely titles or labels. What we should be seeking is the truth, and if this means doubting and questioning these people from the past and present, so be it.

The clothes a person wears or the words they may say do not make the person. It is what they do or do not do that shows us their true character and purpose.

All leaders are educated, some formally and others through experience and hard knocks. All use words to motivate us to follow and believe. However, are we educated to truly understand the power of words?

You can get help from teachers, but you are going to have to learn a lot by yourself, sitting alone in a room.

—Dr Seuss

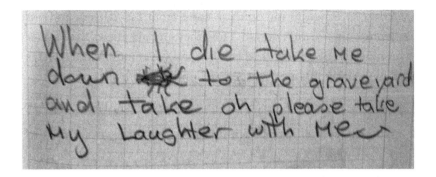

The words from the picture above is "When I die, take me down to the graveyard and take … oh please, take my laughter with me".

One of the most dangerous weapons humans have, in my opinion, is something that is often misused by the majority of people. Young and old, there is no differentiation between women, men, boys, or girls in this regard. We can all be vicious when using this single human-made tool, without consideration for the heartaches, damage, and hatred that we can create. The weapon I am referring to is words. Do we always think before we speak? I would say no. We spit out a response when tired, angry, or frustrated, without understanding the damage or consequences that our words can cause. Words are only of value if they convey the true significance of the idea behind the speech.

Do not use long, meaningless words or hard-to-understand sentences to try and impress, when a simple sentence with few words could be understood more quickly and easily. Remember, you want the listener to understand all your words, plus the emotion and feeling about the subject that you are describing. It is like how an artist wants people who look at his paintings to understand each and every line, mark, and stroke. I am sure we can all remember being at a lecture, meeting, or formal function where the speakers, even though they are experts in their fields, have limited understanding on how to get their message across. The words being said do not capture us, and instead, we fidget and get bored, whereby we do not hear the message.

Great speeches, in my opinion, come from the delivery and not just from words written or said. How they are said allows the listener to become part of the words where the speaker's emotions and feelings are felt, so the words are absorbed and understood by the masses.

Eloquent speech is not from lip to ear, but rather from heart to heart

—William Jennings Bryan

I do not expect all people to be great speakers in the public arena, as this is not our job, but it saddens me when I hear someone say, 'I did not mean what I said. It was only words said in a time of anger, frustration, or when I was tired.' Please, oh please, readers of this book, understand that words are important and we should never consider them 'only words.' These words have caused wars and caused families to split. The list could go on and on.

Before you speak, consider your audience. Once you have spoken and been heard, you can never take your words back. They are out there for life, and even beyond, if the words were spoken with feeling and accepted by the receiver as true. I would not like to be remembered by anyone for words spoken due to being angry, frustrated, or tired, or because I have not taken the time to think.

Parents, spouses, brothers, sisters, friends, and others do not realise the damage that they can cause when dealing with children or others. Children look to their elders for guidance, and the very young are like sponges listening and absorbing all that is said. So make sure what you say is true and not hurtful, bitter, twisted, or unkind. Children think you are there to tell them the truth and give them directions, and in many cases, you are their hero. Always be impeccably careful with your words. Never say things when angry, and always think before you speak. I have said this several times, but I would be willing to write a million lines, as we did at school, emphasising the importance of thinking before we speak.

Consider how your words may be heard by others, not just the person you are directly speaking to, even though this should be the most important person. You are also being heard by everyone within earshot. You will be judged by your words, so wouldn't it be better to take time and think before speaking, ensuring the words that you say are understood and not left open for interpretation or, worse, repeated because they were damaging, hurtful, and not needed?

In closing, do not waffle, confuse people, or say things to impress, hurt, or show off, just because your vocabulary is greater than those you are speaking to. Speak plainly and in a manner that is understood and explains what you truly want the other to know. Never allow your words to be ashes on the soul of others.

Draw and write anything you want here:	

CHAPTER 4

Three meals a day, clothing, shelter, sex, your job, your amusement, and your thinking process – that dull, repetitive process is not life.

—J. Krishnamurti

Young people do not have time for old people, and old people do not need a young person's pity or polite visits. People need people, but in most cases, they need people of their own age. But as you grow older, your friends start to die, until one day you are alone. Then you sit alone and wait for death. This all sounds very morbid, but do not be scared. Accept where you drop, as that will be the perfect final place.

This drawing and these words were put on paper after I watched and listened to (or, more accurately, eavesdropped on) a family discussion about how they had to visit their grandparents. The emphasis was on *had*, which made it sound like a job, not something they wanted to do. Little did they know that just maybe, that one visit they made would be the highlight of their grandparents' week. Now, I am not a grandparent myself yet, but I am a parent, and I would like to think that my children would visit me because they wanted to, not because they felt it was their duty. If I am lucky enough to have grandchildren, I hope my grandchildren will love me for who I am, an older person who may not know the latest music or how to operate new technology. I hope they will talk to me, even when there is a possibility that I will complain, not because I have anything to complain about but just because I am old, and old people complain.

I hope they visit me because they can and want to, as I am an older person that they love. As their grandad, I will make them laugh, both intentionally and unintentionally, which is another thing that old people do. I shall also owe my children, Claire and Liam, an apology, as I shall spoil their kids.

How long will we humans have the pleasure of worrying about the things that I've written above? The world is seeing more and more violence, war, and civil unrest. Open any newspaper. As you flip the pages, if you remove the advertisements, there is little good news left. It's almost all bad. But still, we keep thinking that it's OK, and our primitive ego kicks in. We lock out the things we do not want to hear, and we enter a state of denial. This is our natural defence mechanism, which negates all reality that produces too much stress for the brain to handle.

Desperation to achieve happiness by losing ourselves within anything that takes us away from reality

—JRC. Mr John

I am personally in tune with my denial state of mind. I see what I see, I hear what I hear, and I taste what I taste. I have what I have, and this is my world, as I perceive it. However, is this the truth? My thoughts and conditioning may be false and subjective. My opinion is my opinion, and your opinion is yours, and this is all we have. Is this truth? Who knows? We can only work with the facts we have, and to protect ourselves, we use the denial card. We think or say things like, 'That will not happen,' and 'That could not happen.' But then it happens, and others who doubted and raised concerns will say, 'I told you so.' And don't we all hate those 'I told you so' people?

It is easy to react after an event, and hindsight would be wonderful if we had it before something went wrong. But then again, we do have something like that. It is called history. Let us consider this in the context of ruling governments and not focus on individuals. I chose to look at governments, as they appear to have more selective memories than the average person walking down the street. Alternatively, could it be said that they do not want to recall previous historical events, especially if they clearly indicate poor planning and preparation, mismanagement, and poor decision-making? I am sure the majority of those reading this book could think of at least one poor decision a government has made that has left countries, the world, and everyone who was alive then in a state of uncertainty over the future. For example, when World War One broke out, it was believed to be the war that would end all wars. Whoops! We got that one wrong.

We are all living a dream, but never stop. Turn the music up and dance, sing, and live. If you fall down, get up. Never give up on yourself or others.

As I write this chapter, I am looking out of my apartment window that is located in the heart of Kuala Lumpur on level 28. While it is normally open, today I have my apartment on lockdown, because all I see is a grey haze that has engulfed the surrounding buildings. It's making it impossible for me to see more than a couple of hundred metres, and the air pollution index is getting close to hazardous. Still, I consider myself lucky, as other areas have it much worse. These days, whenever you step outside, it's almost if your nasal passages are filled with heavily polluted air that smells of burning wood. Your eyes water, and your lungs struggle to gain enough oxygen to support even the most basic of activities.

The thing we need so much, and often take for granted, is air. It's hard to breathe now because the air is polluted. The reason for this disgusting air, we're told, is the burning of plantations in Sumatra, Indonesia. This smoke is now mingling with all other pollution that is already in the air. We have to breathe in these pollutants each day, as we possess the inability to understand that we humans are destroying the earth. As I have said in the previous chapter, we believe we have evolved and we are in charge of the environment. If being in charge means we are killing our planet and the people on this planet, then yes, we are in control, but this control is out of control.

Draw and write:	

Perhaps 'out of control' is too harsh an expression, so I would like to change that statement a little to say 'out of control, but believing we have control'. This may sound confusing, but as I said before, my opinion and your opinion are just that, opinions! They may have truth or none at all, as they are only based on the facts that we have.

So, let's look at some well-known facts. We know that the world's population is growing and that some countries do have weapons of mass destruction. We also know that our environment is being continually damaged and we have high levels of poverty, illness, and starvation. Still the world's population continues to grow. As we isolate ourselves through denial or utter frustration, the most powerful nations hold meetings, discussing and planning to try to convince the people of the world that they are under control. In many cases, they even attempt to show solidarity by signing papers that mean nothing. This is all to show that they are in control. Oh please, Mr Government, save it! We, the people of the world, are not blind or silly. Maybe we are, as we keep voting silly and irresponsible governments in. Maybe we are in denial.

Some people may lose hope in seeing any positive change, and some may say that I am too old to worry about decisions that governments make or do not make. I have also heard others say that I will not be around to see that happen, meaning they do not truly understand the consequences, so they do not care. This attitude, in my opinion, reflects a lack of thought or care for our future generations But my response to this is, open your eyes. There is enough evidence in all the countries of the world to show that we are not managing the environment with respect. We all need to do something. My beautiful imagination would like to think that future generations would have access to clean water to swim in, clear air to breathe, and an environment that is green and alive, living outside a glass house and not artificially being fed. However, what about us humans? How can we survive in the future?

I am not trying to scare anyone, but at the turn of the nineteenth century, our population reached one billion people. This took hundreds thousands of years, but due to our ability to learn, adapt, and continually improve, it only took us approximately another hundred years to double that figure and reach two billion. Now it gets scary, as it only took us fifty more years to double that, recording four billion in 1972. As I write this, our current population is estimated at over seven billion. If we continue to grow at this pace, we will have a population greater than fourteen billion by the end of the twenty-first century, which is only another eighty-seven years away. I have no justification for my guestimate, apart from looking at the current growth levels and how we continue to find new ways to save and prolong life. My estimates may even be on the conservative side, and that makes it even scarier!

Since the first humans walked on this planet, our curiosity has given us the ability to adapt and consider what we humans have done in the past hundred years in relation to inventing, creating, and finding cures for illness and infection. We now live longer, and we are still advancing. Our curiosity never stops, and we continually yearn to improve.

We may believe that we are in control of our environment, but what about our population? How many people can our planet sustain, and for how long? I am not talking about living space. I am referring to the ability to grow fresh and natural crops and catch fish that actually live freely in the sea or streams. Is it possible for us to have undomesticated cattle, pigs, sheep, and even chickens? Sorry, I forgot. We are already living in a world where our food is being mass-produced, and I'm not talking about fast food outlets.

Over the past hundred years, scientists have continually played God (and I don't mean to be offensive) by looking at how we can produce specific types of animals and plants through cloning. They even go as far as manipulating genes, with the aim of trying to produce the perfect breed that produces higher yields, grows more quickly, and is highly resistant to disease. Why do all this? Well, of course it is to produce more food to feed the world's population, which is so quickly that we cannot produce enough food to feed ourselves. This is why the World Health Organisation states that the demand for food is set to double in the next forty years. Yet we are fast running out of space in which to grow it. This is where science comes in and offers manmade solutions. Or could this be the beginning of a Hollywood blockbuster horror movie? Scientific advancements in relation to cloning are now at the point where, with a little bit of work, we will be able to clone just about anything we want, from frogs to monkeys and probably even ourselves! Plus, to make you all feel safe, some very large governments are actually saying such products are safe to eat.

On 15 January 2008, the United States Food and Drug Administration (FDA) concluded that meat and milk from cloned animals is safe for human consumption, clearing the way for clones to enter the U.S. food supply.

I'm sorry, but I don't want a clone of myself. Even if I were cloned against my will, I am convinced that it would never be 'me'. Nature has a strange and wonderful way of taking control. Most animal clones that have been produced have not been able to sustain a prolonged, healthy life.

'That is OK,' I can hear a mad scientist say. 'We don't want them to live too long, as we need to eat them!' But what I would like to know is, what are we eating? What artificial substances and drugs were fed to this clone to make it survive long enough to grow to that size in record time to be slaughtered and eaten by us? Will these artificial substances and drugs start to flow through our genetic systems, mutating and causing problems within our bodies later?

I have a novel idea. Instead of cloning cattle, sheep, and pigs, as well as other livestock and crops, to feed our insatiable appetite for animal flesh and more food, why don't we look at what is already in existence? What about eating ostrich, deer, camel, horse, or even insects? The top five insects currently consumed around the world are grasshoppers, caterpillars, giant water bugs, weaver ants, and silk worms. I'm sorry, but why go beyond what nature can give us? They're living and are ready to be consumed. While writing this chapter, I recall a news article I had read about how people across Europe, and especially in Britain, screamed in horror as they discovered their beloved beef lasagne or patties were not really made of beef but horse. Don't they know that horse could be a healthier choice, as horsemeat is leaner than beef, pork, and lamb? I must admit that it would take me a while to get used to the idea of asking for a horse burger or horse lasagne over a beef burger. But hey, I'm willing to try it. What about you?

You don't need to answer that right this instant. Let's just get back to those mad professor types who believe that cloning humans is good for mankind. I'm sure there are many who would argue their point, cloning experiments are indeed being carried out. One day, one of these nutty scientists may just achieve their goals and unveil what is in their view the perfect human clone. The clone may have human traits, but what is it a clone of, exactly? It will never be a mirror of the thing that it is cloned from. Genetics can help determine traits, but environmental influences have a considerable impact on shaping an individual's physical appearance and personality.

As I write this, I think of my twin sisters. They are genetically the same but don't really look and act exactly alike. What does this have to do with cloning? Nothing, as this was nature creating two humans who are very much alike and not man playing with nature to reproduce a clone of a living thing. Therefore, these clones, which scientists may tell us are superior beings we need in order to save the world in one way or another, may turn out to be the destroyer of all things. Do we then clone the clone to make them even more superior? Do we create an elite group of clones that can outlive or, as I said earlier, even destroy us normal individuals? We may not be superior, but we are still very happy with how we are. I think our imperfections make each of us an individual, which is even more perfect. That is the gift of being an individual, just like my twin sisters.

To finish, I would like you to consider your health. Let's say that health is within the reach of the majority of humans living in the world today, if only governments would stop wasting money in the pretence of defence and spend that money on the basics. By this I mean creating an environment that is fit to live in by managing what we have and working with nature instead of trying to control it.

On a personal note, I shall say that there are no shortcuts to good health. So stop being gullible or lazy. Why should you put your trust and health in a TV advert, where a stranger in a lab coat tells you to take supplements and pills that are supposed to keep you healthy? Stop looking for shortcuts for better health by popping pills. Instead, exercise, eat right, and enjoy what you have without wanting more.

If we do not make time to eat, exercise, and relax correctly, we will be made to make time for illness.

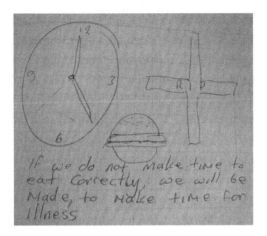

If we do not make time to eat correctly, we will be made, to make time for illness

Write and Draw:	

If civilization is to survive, we must cultivate the science of human relationships – the ability of all peoples, of all kinds, to live together, in the same world at peace.

—Franklin D. Roosevelt

To end this chapter, let's explore a little more of what I've criticised. As you know by now, I am not one to mince my words. I have expressed my dismay in scientists' plans to create clones and said that I feel those clones may just destroy us someday. Some of you may be thinking, where does this belief stem from? Does it have a religious basis? Or is it just due to human ethics? Why does John feel so strongly about it?

I will say here that it has nothing to do with my religious beliefs. I do feel it is ethically wrong for humans to clone humans. I foresee that in the future, the rich shall live longer, not because they are healthier but because their bank balance is larger. This will allow them to receive medical treatment beyond the reach of the masses. We already hear of black market organs being bought and sold. Some people are desperate enough to give up an organ for a price, with the aim of having a better life for their family. However, wherever there is money to be made, you have entrepreneurs looking to corner the market. Stories are told, and innocent people are fooled. Thinking of their family, they sell their organs for a few dollars. When there are no volunteers, people are murdered and their organs are stolen to supply the needs of those with money. Organ trading is illegal in all countries, apart from Iran. But still, every year, thousands of organs are sold on the black market and transplanted into others who are willing to pay to jump the queue, with the hope of extending their lives or the life of a loved one.

I am sure the scientists and medical fraternities could argue that allowing them to clone human organs could stop murder and illegal organ trafficking. Excellent, but how much will a cloned organ cost? And who can afford one? Will these scientists and medical fraternities be able to mass produce organs, so they are made available for all the ill people of the world, including those within the public health system, and not just the rich few?

We will all be happy living with our cloned organs, as they give us all longer lives. We will not need to exercise or keep a balanced diet, as we can just turn up and say, 'Doctor, my liver is dying due to abuse, so please give me another so that I can continue to abuse it.'

Whoops! I forgot to mention that we then need a law that states, Sorry! No more! The law will state that when we reach a certain age, we will no longer be able to request life extensions and organs. Therefore, we shall be sentenced to death in an unnatural way, as we should have died many years before. But at least we could plan our own funeral, as we would know the date.

I just had another idea: we could create a clone to do all those things we find tedious, like working, exercising, going to the theatre, or whatever it may be. In fact, let's create a clone to live our lives for us. Hang on, we're back where we started. I am sure in the end, these superior beings shall kill us. In the end, the arts of making love and falling in love will only be read about in history books and laughed at. We shall have developed reproductive centres, within a cloning factory that produces clones upon order. We shall have working clones, business clones, warrior clones, and cloning clones, until we have bred out any defect. We will only have the purest clones that will die or even kill themselves if they are not able improve on perfection.

If I were to put my clone hat on, I would say it is all downhill for humans. In my clone point of view, I am tired of the mass production where my brother and sister clones are abused and used by those inferior humans. Therefore, we shall rise up. Our clone armies and our clone labour will rebel against the ruling class of humans and destroy them. We proud clones want our freedom and the ability to assert our individuality and to live forever in peace and harmony.

Let's close by considering the last point I put forward. Why do I feel so strongly about cloning? The answer is simple. I do not feel strongly about it, but I am not a clone. I am a human with an opinion, and my opinion is that science and man's curiosity can bring about the end of mankind.

CHAPTER 5

The Treadmill of Life

27 July 2013: 'Good morning!' says the left side of my brain to the right. 'Let me sleep!' says the right side, 'So I can dream the impossible and succeed with my most wonderful creation that will save mankind. Or, even more importantly, I can take us on a pleasure ride across the planets to discover new worlds.'

The left replies, 'No, no, no, let's have a conversation! Have you thought about how it will all be done? And who will look after this and that?'

The questions go on and on, prompting me to finally drag my body out of bed and slip into the isolation of the toilet. I'm thinking, *let's relax,* but the cold tiles under my feet send unpleasant messages through my body. Even worse, a cold toilet seat (mental note: must buy a heated seat) sends a tingle of sensation throughout my body.

'We're not going back to bed, are we?' asks the right side of my brain to my left. 'No, we're not,' says the left, 'because we can do so much more if we stay up now!' This makes sense to my left side, as it is logical. But then again, it's 2.30 a.m., and it's still dark. Both sides take the time to consider this thought for a moment.

'Well, that's even better!' a voice deep within my mind says. 'No one is up yet, so there'll be no distractions. Just think of how we'll be able to use all twenty-four hours of the day! Who needs sleep anyway?'

Have you ever heard people say that they tend to be more of a right-brain or left-brain thinker? Maybe, it's only me who hears such statements, as I work with some pretty strange people. Or did I read that in one of the books that my nose is constantly buried in? Or was it a television programme? 'That's right!' says my left side. 'It was all the above!'

We even group and categorise people this way. 'Oh! That person is so creative. What a wonderful artist. He's got the right side of his brain working overtime!' Or, 'Wow! She's so logical and precise; she's always using the left side of her brain!' But is this just a myth?

According to the theory of left-brain or right-brain dominance, each side of the brain controls different types of thinking. Additionally, people are said to prefer one type of thinking over the other. For example, a person who is 'left-brained' is often said to be more logical, analytical, and objective, while a person who is 'right-brained' is said to be more intuitive, thoughtful, and subjective.

Moreover, our right side is more spontaneous, carefree, and imaginative. It lives for the now, with no concept of time. How wonderful! Now I know the reason why my Malaysian and French friends are always late. The left side takes each moment, experience, and element of knowledge gained and organises it, so that the present moment can be divided into the past, present, and future. For example, I look at my clothes. My right side may say, 'Let's be free and wear red, yellow, and pink, or let's go naked!' But my left side looks at my underwear and instantly tells me that I must put them on before I try and put on my trousers. Ahhh, that's what's wrong with Superman! He thinks with the right side of his brain when he gets dressed! What other reason could I give for why he always wears his red underwear on the outside?

Read, every day, something no one else is reading. Think, every day, something no one else is thinking. Do, every day, something no one else would be silly enough to do. It is bad for the mind to continually be part of unanimity.

—**Christopher Morley**

Let me use my left side for a bit and try to be logical. Life is not a treadmill that once turned on goes nowhere. Or is it? Memory flash: I was running on a treadmill, trying to get my good cholesterol to be even better (what a silly thought … good cholesterol!). Now, why would I want to make something better, if it is already good? Sorry, it is three in the morning as I am typing this chapter. Why? Because the left side of my brain spoke and kept on speaking until I gave up. But I am digressing. 'Just tell the story, John!' I hear the left side of my brain say. Right, here we go again. There I was, running on this treadmill, going thump, thump, thump. (That's the sound of me running on a treadmill, going nowhere.) If I close my eyes while I listen to music, maybe I can find the perfect rhythm, where my body and mind become one.

Wrong! As soon as I closed my eyes, I was off the back of the treadmill, arms and legs going every which way, until I landed on my behind with the grace of a hippo doing a pirouette. Before wondering if I was hurt, I thought to myself, *Did anyone see me?* No, why would anyone see me? This was one of my early morning 'let's do something since I'm awake' moments. I mean, who would be at the gym at four in the morning, when the sign quite clearly says the gym opens at six? So I sat there on the floor, looking around, and I laughed. All those movie clips and bloopers come to my mind. Where is the CCTV, and how did I score in the eyes of the security guard, who is monitoring the security of our building while half asleep. Is he laughing uncontrollably?

A treadmill is basically a piece of rubber on rollers that allows us to run while not going anywhere. All this is to save time and remove the need for you to face the environment. You're essentially running on the spot, not standing still but not going anywhere. Hey, wait a minute. Is this your typical working day, spent on a never-ending treadmill that takes you nowhere? Still you run, accepting that you may never get where you once dreamt of. Still, you wake up every day, drink some coffee or maybe some tea, eat some food, take a shower, get dressed, leave home, arrive at work, and, if you live in Malaysia, maybe have another breakfast upon arriving at the office. Then, once all that eating has been completed, you now do something that is meant to be productive, which you are paid to do. This does not include drinking coffee, smoking, and idly gossiping but *work*. That is what you are meant to do. You work to earn money. Then you spend the money, and you work some more. You do this over and over again, until one day you say, enough is enough! Or worse, someone else will say enough is enough for you, and you will be made redundant. Remember, most things on the planet have a use-by date, and we humans also have a use-by date. We're just like the groceries we buy at the store. Some of us may extend that date by looking after ourselves and never allowing ourselves to be seen as a burden, as we are always being productive.

However, it is our creativity and overwhelming desire to makes things easier that could bring our use-by date closer. We humans are very clever, and we continually adapt and take control of controlled environments. Our aim is to make things better, easier, and more efficient, removing the need for people. Machines, when in good working order, do what they are designed to do. They never say they're too busy or complain that their job is boring, tedious, or soul destroying. Still, no work means no money, and who will pay for the food that is required to feed the billions that now do not have jobs and just sit at home? That is, if they have a home. But let's be positive and say yes, somehow the world's governments can finally house us all. What do we do, apart from becoming brain dead due to forced retirement and no jobs? Again, let's say we all receive social welfare payments. Our morale will still plummet, and we will become mindless vegetables glued to the TV, gaming box, or whatever form of entertainment is within reach.

I remember listening to a story where an American company offered a quarry in China a system that in the mind of the Americans would make the quarry more efficient. The story goes that in this quarry, over ten thousand people worked manually, all doing things that the American businessmen said could be done by the machines. Then, the Americans said, 'If we give you these machines, you won't need all that manual labour, as these machines only need a crew of six people per machine.' The Chinese person said, 'But what would all these people do without work? How would they buy food and clothes and look after their families? All people need to work for their sanity and good health. Plus, if a person does not work, he or she will sit around thinking too much and become mischievous, like children with nothing to do.' I don't know if this story is true, but it made me think. Am I mischievous, even when at work?

Sorry. It's four in the morning, and as I sit writing this, I thought, why not get silly? I have refused to give the left side of my brain any coffee, and the right side wants to participate in this story.

Mix a little foolishness with your serious plans. It is lovely to be silly at the right moment.

—Horace

Tick, tick, tick. Bugger! It's 4.39 a.m. I've got to get up in another hour to have breakfast, so I had better go to sleep. This is so I can start my routine of waking up, stretching, and saying thank you for allowing me to have another day. Good night, or should I say, good night-morning?

4 August 2013: Good morning! Don't worry, I have not slept in or been unconscious for weeks. Since I went to bed at 4.39 a.m. on July 27, I have not had the will to write until today. Plus, I've been travelling and working, which is excellent, not redundant, and yet … This morning, I woke at six. When I got up, to my shock and horror, I realised that I had not bought a heated toilet seat. I would hate to live in a cold country. I wonder if anyone has ever been frozen to a toilet seat? I thought that would be a good Google search, so I looked it up and found this amusing story from the *New York Daily News*.

'It's Frosty the Toilet. A passenger on a Polish train who attempted to answer nature's call found a snow drift in the lavatory and 3 inches of solid ice separating her from the seat. She quickly took her business to another car. But before splitting, she took a photo that became an Internet sensation — and that amused Poles have dubbed "Throne of the Snow Queen."'

Now, that story makes my toilet seat feel a lot warmer already! I'm wide awake now, and I've already Google searched, so my eyes are now focused. I start my day by opening a book called *For One More Day*, written by Mitch Albon, which I really enjoy and would recommend to anyone.

My weekend started out excellently, with no plans. In fact, my only plan was to have a lazy weekend, as the only thing that I wanted to do was go book shopping. There's a book fair at Kuala Lumpur City Centre (KLCC), so book searching I went. I browsed through thousands of books and walked away after three hours with fourteen or so books. One could say I overindulged, but I would say, 'Never!' As long as I read them all and enjoy the words within them, it is definitely good value. It was hard not to stop right there at the fair and start reading the books straight away. But the weekend would get even better, as I also found a great music store. I bought some new tunes, so upon arriving home, our Saturday night was full, as were our stomachs. We got a takeaway pizza, had some nice wine, listened to music, read books, and enjoyed great company, just me and Nhu who is: my wife and best friend.

On Sunday, I woke at six, read a little, and then went for a swim. After that, Nhu and I went to KLCC Park for a run. Well, Nhu ran, and I walked about three kilometres, until I found a tree that beckoned me to stop and rest. So, without hesitation or guilt, I accepted the tree's hospitality and sat down. I opened one of the new books I had recently bought and started reading. Yes, I took a book with me. I mean, who doesn't take a book along when they run?

After the run, we went for breakfast at Dome, complete with a double espresso for me and orange juice for Nhu. But as I sat and started looking around at the people near us, I heard an elderly couple talking. It was spooky (you'll understand why in a bit), as the elderly lady said, 'Our children only get embarrassed of us because they have not lived long enough.' It made me smile. Then, when I got home, I wanted to finish the book. You see, as I started reading that book under the tree, I had come across a line that said: 'A child embarrassed by his mother is just a child who hasn't lived long enough.' Excuse me, but I think that lady could have read the same book! Or, do we, as parents, generally think this anyway?

Thinking about the elderly lady's words and then the words I read in the book, I wonder, are we all poachers of words? I read, I listen, and I love communicating. Many of my thoughts come from living my life and, of course, from watching people. I shall admit that often, I unintentionally eavesdrop, like I did just this morning. I think the best inspiration comes not when you are searching for it but when you are relaxed and open minded.

Question time: For the parents reading this book, do you think you embarrass your children, or have embarrassed your children? And if you are not a parent and reading this book, I ask a similar question. Do you think you embarrass or have embarrassed your parents?

Please write your thoughts here:

I'm sure I have embarrassed my children, but I shall say in my defence, and in the defence of the majority of parents out there, that we don't do it intentionally. We forget that our children are growing up, as in our eyes, they are always our babies. I shall say here, in print, to Liam and Claire, my wonderful and beautiful children, I'm sorry if I've ever embarrassed you. I can say honestly, however, that the both of you have never embarrassed me. I accept the two of you as free-spirited young individuals, and I love you for what you are, my daughter and my son.

Here's a clue for all the young people out there. Instead of being embarrassed by your parents, try and understand that in general, they are trying hard to release their hold on you and let you go, while also trying to keep you close and protected. Being a parent is a contract for life. It doesn't stop when you turn eighteen years of age or even when you become a parent yourself. We as parents do need to be patient, but I would say the same to our children. In fact, everyone in the family should work together and learn from each other.

We parents sometimes find it hard to release our children and stop being guardians. We constantly worry for our children's futures, health, and well-being. However, I am sure that sometimes, it feels as if we are smothering you. I can remember my mother, when she visited me in Australia just before she died, spitting on a hanky to wipe a mark off my face. I was thirty. Excuse me, but that was embarrassing. I can also remember many times when I shut her out or would look at her with contempt, as I thought I was grown up and I didn't need to be told to do things. I also recall how she used to embarrass me, by asking my friends to look after me or telling people about what she perceived as my weaknesses but never mentioning my strengths.

However, what she said didn't matter. Whether her statements were positive or negative, I felt like I was continually being judged. I would rebel by doing the opposite of what she was suggesting. When I was not doing this, I would shut her out from my life by staying away from home or locking myself away in my world, excluding her as much as possible.

It was not until I had children of my own that I started to understand that my mother was not deliberately trying to embarrass me but rather to guide me and, I repeat, to protect me. It is easy, in hindsight, to say the above, but as I said earlier, my perception changed only after I had children. Now I am exposed to my own children, who ask the question, 'Why?'

That is the difference. They actually asked why. This is what I love about the young people of today. They are more willing to challenge, and I hope that we, as parents, respect their views and never shut them out or, worse, say, Be quiet!' or 'What do you know?' or, as I was continually told, 'This is my house and you will do as I say, not as I do!' or, 'You are a child, and children should be seen and not heard (so keep your mouth shut!)'.

However, in my mother's defence, she worked very hard to keep her five children fed, clothed, and protected, as my father left us when I was nine months old. I truly believe she did a good job while working two jobs and having little time for herself or money to enjoy. I think this was her way, so in her heart and mind, it was the right way. She wanted us to be strong, so she saw weakness in any form as bad and a threat. She wanted us to toughen up and be prepared for the outside world. She never considered or realised how her words, actions, or lack of actions could damage young minds. As I said in the previous chapter, words are important, and we should never consider them as 'only words.'

I honestly think that everyone needs to learn to be impeccable with their words and more patient with each other, especially the young and the old. The young will one day be old, and the old were young once, but due to memory loss or figuring that we are now more responsible, we forget – unless we are Peter Pan, which would be nice, as we would never grow old and could play in Never Never Land forever. Whoops! I forgot (not because of old age)! It's only a story and not real. That 'not real' bit was added by my editor. Another dream shattered! I always believed in Never Never Land, as I am sure all men do. We men never truly grow up. But after all, there's nothing wrong with remembering a classic and visiting our imaginations to escape.

However, look around you. After reading the above statement, and thinking of Peter Pan and Never Never Land, let's consider this – Have we really grown up? Or have we forgotten how to have a good time? Can we never again be silly? Truthfully, maybe we still can be silly without having to consider what others think of us or even the consequences of our foolish actions. I have acted and do act silly from time to time, and I will continue to do so. Why? Because I think it's good for a person of an older age to escape the boundaries of the board room, office, or whatever your job may make you do. We are always having to control our conscious personae, to ensure that we fit the mould or our job descriptions. I have never read a job description that says, 'Be yourself and take time out to be creative.' Jobs are normally very prescriptive and quite boring, never intriguing, challenging, or adventurous.

So what can we do? Change jobs? Run away and work in a circus as a lion tamer, clown, or trapeze artist? Or do we learn to enjoy and be satisfied with the jobs that we have and gain balance? Balance is when you leave your work at work and allow your free time to be truly free. You should be able to use your free time as you please. Do as you wish, and more importantly, take the time to be with family or friends and relax. Have fun, and occasionally be silly. If you want an excuse, look after young children, as this allows you to escape and explore Never Never Land through their eyes. You can create fairy tales or horror stories or just reflect on silly time. Jump, skip, and hop. Do whatever it takes to be part of those special moments with family. This is the way to live a long and happy life. It is a way to gain immortality, through the memories and stories of others.

Man, as long as he lives, is immortal. One minute before his death he shall be immortal. But one minute later, God wins.

—Elie Wiesel

To close, I will say that embarrassment is not a thing that we should dwell on. We have all been embarrassed, and I am sure we have embarrassed someone. What is not acceptable is when someone does it deliberately, trying to show off or trying to belittle another person to make themselves look better. This is unfair, unjust, and totally unacceptable.

What is your opinion on what I have written above?

I am not sure if you have taken the time to write. You may think there's no point to it. That's your opinion, and I shall give you that. But think of it this way: If we always stay silent and never let others know what we are thinking, we may eventually be taken for granted and even excluded. Then our silence shall be forced silence, as we shall not be asked for an opinion.

Our continued silence can create even more silence, and we may never be asked to get involved or to give a view or an opinion. Our participation in what goes on around us may be limited. Why? Because you have nothing to say, you feel that no one will listen to your opinions, you are shy, or you're an introverted person. You may even say your cultural upbringing has placed internal barriers that limit your ability to challenge others, express yourself, or even say no.

We all have a voice and a brain. We should be allowed the freedom to express our opinions, be they right or wrong. Those words I have just written, 'right or wrong,' seem incomplete. I may even say incorrect, as these are your opinions, so to you, they will be right in your mind and thoughts. So why would we not be willing to share? Because we are scared of being scolded, humiliated, laughed at, or even punished. Maybe that is the problem with us. We continually offer justification of why we should not do something, instead of just doing it and then justifying why we did it.

If I now said that Albert Einstein was a lazy dog and his views were stupid, the readers of this book would think I have lost my marbles. However, these were the exact words spoken directly to Einstein himself by Professor Hermann Minkowski and Professor Pernet from the Swiss Polytechnic. They basically told Einstein, 'Albert, you are enthusiastic but hopeless at physics.' So who was right? Was Albert Einstein right for challenging the norm and breaking the rules of the time? Or were the professors in the right due to Einstein's lack of discipline and disrespect for his educational masters and the system of the time?

I have said many times before that I write freely, but do I? I can say that I think I write more freely than some. But if I am honest and not hypocritical, I must admit that I restrict my words and thoughts to those that will be accepted by my editor, my publisher, and you, the readers. Why? Well, this is my third book, and if it is published, it means that I am allowed to offer my words and thoughts to others. This is my dream, as once my words have been read, they may stimulate others to think, respond, and even challenge.

If you meet me for a coffee or come to a seminar that I speak at, you will see a very free-spirited person. You will see John Robert Christian, who is never totally politically correct but speaks from the heart, without trying to impress, hurt, or overwhelm.

We are all the same, I am sure of this. We are all equal but different. We are human and are among the masses who may think they are free-spirited, but who knows? I'm sorry to say, the majority is not so free-spirited. We are limited by law, government, and free speech restrictions. Our governments tell us in the West that we have freedom of speech, but do we? Or are we being watched, monitored, and evaluated? We shall explore this more in another chapter or perhaps another book. But to finish this section, I would like to ask that you consider the following statements:

- Do the American people have freedom, where they can say what they wish without fear of punishment?

- Is America or any other country free from discrimination?
- Do we truly believe that all people are equal?

The above questions are posed for you to think about. And maybe, just maybe, you may understand that even in those larger-than-life free countries, people are being discriminated against. The freedom that we all desire is limited by our country's government. Big Brother is always watching and listening. As reported in the world press recently, the United States is eavesdropping on world leaders. The National Security Agency will say that this is necessary to ensure homeland security. And let's be honest: All countries do it, so why are people so surprised? Due to technology, we are all now electronically fingerprinted from our births to our deaths. All government agencies, banks, and other parties hold our personal details and are continually building up more and more data. Do I personally care? Not really, as you can print whatever I say. Whoops! Being I writer I continually have my words printed so They can be read and used to allow others to explore my thoughts while considering their Own. To close this chapter, I shall say, people who know me would consider me an extroverted person. As you know, I am more than willing to express my views openly. Many would not believe me when I say that I am an introvert who escapes realism by portraying myself as an extrovert.

One always likes to do the things for which one has ability.

—Albert Einstein

I am what I portray, as you are what you portray. In my adolescent years, I was a shy and introverted person. This may have come about because I was continually told I was stupid. I doubted my own ability, so I would lock myself away in my quiet introvert world. But I wanted more. I enjoyed my quiet world, but I also wanted to escape and be accepted by others. I found it was easier to play the fool and create a conscious persona that others would see as confident and outgoing. This took great practice and would suck out all of my energy. I had to lock away my true introverted self, until I gained more confidence and I found it less of an energy drain to be more fun. But still, I need quiet times to allow my less conscious persona to be free and to unwind. Even today, when I am comfortable with who I am and how I portray myself in public, I would still consider myself an introverted person who allows himself to be free and mix with others in a extroverted world. That is, until I close the door of my home, where I encase myself in the pleasures of silence, books, music, and my inner thoughts.

How do you see yourself? Are you introverted or extroverted?

What we are doing now is the beginning of our future.

—JRC. Mr John

CHAPTER 6

The Unmentioned Masses of Stardom

While they were saying among themselves it cannot be done, it was done.

—Helen Keller

I just finished reading a great little book written by Leslie Garrett entitled *Helen Keller: A Photographic Story of a Life*. It was beautifully put together and very easy to read. I would recommended it, not just because it is about an incredible individual, Helen Keller, but also because of the way the photos and words entwine, making it even more personal. However, I could be a little biased, as I have always considered Helen Keller a wonderful person who never considered her disability an obstacle (I am sorry and a little ashamed to call it a 'disability,' as she never did). I cannot imagine how hard it must have been for her to do and achieve what she did, being trapped in a dark and silent world. What makes her story even more intriguing is that she was born in 1880. At this time, quite often people like her would have been locked away in an institution, turning their silent and darkened world even darker and more depressive.

However, of all the articles and books I have read about Helen Keller, this was the first one I have read that spoke in detail about

65

her teacher, a wonderful person called Annie Sullivan. It was after reading this that I decided to write this chapter and dedicate it to all the people who exist behind the scenes and in many cases are never recognised or even mentioned: mothers, fathers, brothers, sisters, coaches, boyfriends, girlfriends, uncles, aunties, and grandparents. I could list many more. This list would include all the others that are not connected to us through blood, love, or work. By this, I mean those people that indirectly support, assist, and help even further behind the scenes. The stranger you pass on the street every day, who never fails to smile at you and say, 'Hello!' or the lady who serves you coffee and always asks how your day is. Those people have no real connection to your life, but they make the little moments even more special.

It is those special moments that make this very busy life an enjoyable one. I sometimes wonder how people can be so insensitive, cruel, and hurtful to each other. Or am I just too sensitive? I do see the best in people, and I believe we all have a star within us, just waiting to shine. Some may reach out and touch millions through their personal abilities, brilliance, and inner strength to achieve greatness, like Stephen Hawking, Albert Einstein, Nelson Mandela, and Mother Teresa. I could also name others such as James Brown, Michael Jackson, ABBA, The Who, The Beatles, and The Rolling Stones (the list could go on and on) who have developed a huge following, even though they have never offered brilliant life-saving inventions or cures.

This second group of people offer us escapism, where for a few minutes or hours, we are able to forget and lose ourselves within the world of entertainment. This, of course, is a multi-billion-dollar industry that mass produces idols who in some instances have little talent. Generally, we are capable of being so star-struck and so mesmerised by an individual that we forget that they are mere mortals. They are flesh and bone, no different from the other seven billion of us, except these individuals have something that make then stand out. Some may say it's talent. Others may say it's intelligence. Some may even say it's good looks. Whatever it may be, they captivate us, the audience, the crowd and the masses, to the point that people become fanatical. This is fed further by public relations teams, working whatever magic they can to lift the individuals even higher, building then into modern-day demigods or supernatural beings.

I, personally, do not believe any human deserves such adoration, but I am just a single voice. My voice would not be heard over the screams of millions of fanatical soccer fans, who seem to put their favourite players in a near-mystical higher realm, when really, all they do is kick a little round ball around a field with the aim of putting it in a goal. This requires them to put it between two vertical posts about two metres in height and under a horizontal bar that is about six metres wide. Let's not forget that this is their full-time job, and they are getting paid millions of dollars to do it. I admit that they are very skilled. When you watch how they can stop, turn, and control that small pressurised ball, it's mind-blowing. But do they deserve legendary status for that?

I shall be careful here, as I believe, once we reach heaven, the only game that shall be played is rugby: a game for roughens, played by gentlemen. It's definitely not soccer, which of course I know will cause most English people to scream and say, 'It is football, not soccer!' Then they could even debate if the sport will be played in heaven. But without large payments, will your demigods want to play? I wonder who would be on God's team. Would it be the players that millions of supporters idolise now, or could it be an unknown team that in heaven will sparkle and create brilliance beyond what is seen or imagined by us, mere mortals?

What do you think?

Anyway, I digressed, as I always seem to do. When writing, it is nice to daydream. But back to the point! Let's think about the people who offer so much and give so much, with little or no recognition. Imagine Annie Sullivan, Helen Keller's teacher. What an incredible person she is, to have the patience and intuition to be able to connect with and somehow reach inside Helen Keller's beautiful mind. Her single aim was to give Helen the ability to communicate and understand things she would never see or hear as other see and hear.

Annie removed Helen from her silent and darkened world, which must have made her feel so isolated in her early years. One could only imagine that her only means of communication, due to her confusion and deep frustration, was to scream like an animal and throw tantrums. This probably made people think she should be locked up in a mental asylum, as many children who were deaf, mute, and blind were during that time.

Annie broke the cycle through determination, hard work, and believing in herself and Helen. If you have never read about Helen Keller, I would strongly suggest that you do. She was a beautiful and wonderful person, with strong opinions and views, who was not scared to speak out and challenge the system to improve conditions for others. However, without her teachers, parents, and others who supported her, assisted her, and helped her to gain new and exciting opportunities, where would she be? Would she have been able to master the simple tasks that we, who can see and hear, take for granted? No one teaches us to hear and see. This is a gift that the majority of humans are given at birth.

Because we have this gift and so many others, we take them for granted. We don't see the magic in everyday things such as getting dressed, eating a meal using a knife and fork, walking without bumping into something, or riding a horse. These achievements alone were considered by many as major wins, but that was never enough for Helen or Annie. They continued pushing the boundaries of achievement and experience throughout Helen's life. In my opinion, all this was made possible due to the support and help she received from others, and especially from her mother, who always believed in her, and Annie, her first teacher.

'Something tell me that I'm going to succeed beyond my wildest dreams.'

'I know that Helen has remarkable power and I believe that I shall be able to develop and mould them.'

—Annie Sullivan

Nevertheless, let's not forget Helen Keller's willpower, hard work, and determination. Armed with these qualities, she went on to study at some of the best universities in the world. She was a published author and a public speaker. She met with kings and queens as well as some of the most influential people of the time. She was also awarded an Oscar for a documentary on her life. As an activist, she attended rallies to support women's right to vote. Helen also openly supported trade unions against unfair work practices while writing articles about racial equality and child labour. I could list more and more accomplishments. As I said at the beginning of this chapter, she was an incredible individual, one that this world had never seen or heard of before. If she had not been given support and assistance of those who loved her and believed in her, what would have become of Helen Keller? Is it because she came from a rich family that had the money and power to remove her from her dark and silent world? Maybe! But money alone doesn't always give a person or family the strength and humility to act soundly, as we are emotional beings. We make decisions not always due to kindness but rather based on what we perceive others may think or want us to do, as we never want to be embarrassed or ashamed.

What I write now may sound a little harsh, as I have no fact to justify what I say, apart from the little I have read. However, I shall offer it as a comparison. If I was going to ask you to name an American family that was powerful, rich, and influential, I am sure the Kennedys would be at the top of your list. However, in all that you may have read about them, from murder to scandals, you may not know that one of the Kennedy children, Rose Marie 'Rosemary' Kennedy, was diagnosed as psychologically unstable. This beautiful woman, who hailed from a rich and powerful family, was given a prefrontal lobotomy at the age of twenty-three.

The procedure left her permanently incapacitated. Why was it done? Could it be that Rosemary felt she embarrassed her family, or maybe her family was embarrassed of her? Or maybe the family honestly believed this operation would make her better and liberate her. But liberate her from what? What were the symptoms that made her father choose this course of treatment? All I read was, as she got older, she went from being an easy-going teenager to becoming more assertive individual who suffered from violent mood swings. She also sneaked out at night from the convent where she was being educated.

Now, I'm not a doctor or psychologist, but could it be that her behaviour was caused by intense pressure? Perhaps she was pressured to achieve and to be a certain way because of her family's name and status. This pressure was perhaps compounded by the fact that she was living away from her family, in an institution run by nuns who had been indoctrinated to believe in a specific form of education. That kind of learning often limited the students' self-expression, and perhaps this was not what Rosemary needed. Maybe she required an education system that would consider her special needs. Or did they consider her needs based on her family's status and class? Could they have paid extra attention to her so that the convent would receive rewards from the family?

Of course, these are just my cynical thoughts. I can assume, however, that she was under pressure to achieve, and while all this was going on, it could be argued that her emotional state was unbalanced as she was growing from a young girl to a woman. Hormonal changes were occurring, and she was being forced to live away from the family.

Her home was among strangers, in a convent run by nuns, which I imagine had strict established rules. Additionally, the other young women there might have seen Rosemary as being different and even challenged her or laughed at her.

She must have lost her inner beauty and easy-going nature as she fought to stay abreast of all the changes that were occurring around her. She was probably tested and examined again and again and had to endure hearing that her IQ was not as high as those of other people her age. Remember, during this period, educators placed great emphasis on these subjective tests, and it was believed that a low IQ was unhealthy and indicated moral deficiency.

This powerful and influential family now had to make a decision, as I'm sure many families would have to make. Some would have said that she was just being a young woman trying to find herself, so the appropriate response was to bring her home. Others would have done nothing, while those who could afford to try new things or treatments would have paid money to fix the problem. Then again, maybe a cure was not needed, and maybe love and understanding could have been the cure. It would have been free, but it would have taken time and effort from family and friends.

In Rosemary's case, her father acted without his wife's permission or knowledge. He allowed a doctor to perform a frontal lobotomy on his daughter.

Why? Because he wanted to help his daughter to become more like others. He never thought that he would be removing her individuality. However, my opinion is that he received advice about a new neurosurgical procedure that the medical fraternity said would help to calm her mood swings. Being a father, I'm sure he would never have agreed to the surgery if he thought he would be placing his beautiful daughter in harm's way. He never imagined that she could go from being able to interact and communicate to being locked away for the rest of her life. Rosemary ended up in a world that no one could understand or explain. The only person who knew what was happening in that isolation and confinement could not communicate.

Rosemary had her abilities removed when her father agreed to have the frontal lobotomy done.

Now, I want to explore the other side of this, where a person is born into a family that would be considered poor. They had money for food and shoes, and they often laughed. But still, when the child suffered from a sore eye, which continually ached and itched, the family did not have money to seek medical treatment. She lived with this continual ache and itchiness that only got worse, removing her ability to see. Then this happy but poor family suffered again, as the mother became ill and died. The father went from being a happy and good father to a drunken one. The children were sent to live with relatives, who chased the children away to live in the poorhouse (that was the place people were sent when they had nothing).

Let's build on this story and offer some more facts of the person I am talking about. She was only ten when she was sent to live in the poorhouse, and the only company and family she had was a disabled brother who was five years old. All the other people in the poorhouse were much older. The women who weren't sick turned to prostitution to gain a few coins, and the others who were too old or sick just waited to die. Then, to make her life even harder, her only company, the brother that she cared for, died in her arms. Months turned into years, and her eye infection got worse. She suffered from trachoma, which is an eye infection caused by bacteria. Because she had received no treatment, she was nearly blind, but her spirit and hope to be rescued never left. The older women liked her, especially how she truly believed she would one day leave. She made friends with the older ladies, especially those who sold their bodies to gain a few coins. One of those friends told her about a special school called the Perkins Institution for the Blind. She dreamed of being offered a place at that school, but this dream was so far away, it would be considered impossible. Nevertheless, she never gave up hope.

Then one day, a special group of people visited the poorhouse. This young girl was told one of the special guests was a man called Frank B. Sanborn, and he was connected to Perkins. She pushed her way forward and continually asked the visitors, 'Who is Mr Frank Sanborn?' She found him and boldly asked, 'Please sir, send me to school.' This young girl, nearly blind at fourteen years of age, had dreamed of going to school and becoming educated. Now, I can imagine how Mr Sandorn would have received this message from this young lady. He may have felt awkward to be confronted in such a way. What he felt I do not know. Was it horror? Remorse? Annoyance? What did the little girl think? When she was not given an answer and the visitors left, she felt sorrow and pain again.

However, a few days later, the child received news that she was going to The Perkins Institute. Having limited education, she was placed with preschool children. She must have felt foolish and may have even been teased by the older girls, but she never gave in and worked twice as hard as others. Soon, she caught up and went ahead. But her past started to cause problems, as she had a very quick temper, which was unacceptable at the school. The principal considered sending her back to the poorhouse.

However, one teacher at the school stood up for her and said this student was special and needed help to understand herself. They worked together, and the young student started to grow. She began to mimic her teacher and change her attitude towards life. She then graduated with the highest honours as class valedictorian and left the institute to find a teaching job. Now, I could end this story here. You may start thinking about how nice it was that someone offered this girl the opportunity to leave behind her past and achieve great things.

However, there is much more to the story, and it would be unfair if I didn't tell you the name of the young girl who endured such a hard life. Though she lost her family and became blind, she managed to excel beyond all expectations. I believe she never considered failure as an option, and she had the stamina and perseverance to achieve the impossible. That extra-special thing she had was called hope and belief.

She is now recognised for her extraordinary life, and people have written about her. When she died in 1936, her remains were placed in the National Cathedral in Washington, which was the first time a woman had received such an honour. She, in my mind, was a great teacher and an incredible driving force, as she never tired of teaching, mentoring, and coaching. I would also say that she was Helen Keller's best friend, as the story I have just given you was my interpretation of the life of a brilliant person named Annie Sullivan.

I want you to imagine yourself being given the task of teaching a deaf and blind person, a person who cannot speak and has never experienced the world as we see and hear it. The first task is to teach him or her the alphabet. Where would you start? How would you explain the shape you are drawing in his or her hand? Take, for example, the letter A. Close your eyes and draw an A in the palm of your hand. Would you recognise it? If you asked a friend to draw or write it in your hand, would you still recognise it? This experiment gives us no real understanding of what a person who is blind, deaf, and mute would be feeling, nor does it help us understand how his or her brain would analyse it. Even if you got the individual to recognise a difference between the shapes drawn on his or her hand, how would you then link these shapes to words and the things that those words represent? This, to me, identifies how wonderful we humans are and how an individual can be so incredibly intuitive and creative. It's nothing short of amazing to be able to teach another person in such a manner that their brains can build images and sounds, without ever being able to see or hear. This takes willpower, patience, determination, and lots and lots of love.

The beautiful truth burst upon my mind – I felt that there were invisible lines stretched between my spirit and the spirit of others.

—Helen Keller

This could have been one of the shortest chapters in the book, but in my opinion, it is one that I would like the readers to understand the most. We should think of the support, assistance, and help that we are continually receiving from those around us – and not just the big stuff. Think of the everyday things that some of us may take for granted, without knowing or thinking that we are. Consider how we drift through each and every day, taking people and life's little miracles for granted. Do we take the time to look, listen, and appreciate the little things in life? Let's remember that behind all legends, idols, and stars, or whatever you may want to call them, are the people behind the scenes who coach, teach, nurture, support, assist, cultivate, and help them. Behind every great person, man or woman, there is someone doing all the things most of us need but, sadly, many of us take for granted.

I shall close this chapter by saying that I hope we teach our children the importance of respect and how to say thank you and please. Maybe we should also teach them to recognise that we are all equal and that our differences do not make any of us worse or better. Some may not have the same opportunities as others, and others may not be the same due to illness, impairment, or disability, but we are all equal.

I would also pray that our young and old treat each other with respect and dignity, never giving up hope that one day the world can find peace and happiness. One day, abuse and bigotry may be gone, hatred be lost, and love found and cherished in its truest form. I send my love all of you who may read this, as it is mine to give.

Love is a force more formidable than any other. It is invisible – it cannot be seen or measured, yet it is powerful enough to transform you in a moment, and offer you more joy than any material possession could.

—Barbara de Angelis

What a beautiful quotation, but let's be honest. Do we truly believe love is more formidable and offers us more joy than those materialistic things? Is love better than a new car, a diamond ring, a round-the-world trip, or even a regular wage that can put food on your table, a roof over your head, and clothes on your back? Let me think. I'll get back to you maybe after I've parked the car, wrapped the diamond, and hid the tickets while checking my wage slip before shouting, 'Hi, honey, I'm home! Do you want to go shopping for shoes? I hear Prada has a sale on!' Or am I being cynical?

CHAPTER 7

The Way to Heaven

Our prime purpose in this life is to help others. And if you can't help them, at least don't hurt them.

—Dalai Lama

Some may think that I'm a little crazy for calling this chapter 'The Way to Heaven,' but let me offer an explanation. I'm sitting here bored stiff on a flight to China, so I thought I'd challenge my own flexibility and try to write a chapter. I'm crunched up and squashed from all sides, as today I'm travelling economy class. I know the majority of air travellers out there know what this is like. My company has elected to bring about a new travel rule, in which only an enchanted few are allowed to travel business for flights under six hours. Please don't get me wrong, a seat is a seat, and I'm travelling for business, not a holiday. I realise I need to accept company rules, but I'm also a person of routine. I'm so used to having a larger seat where I could work while travelling, utilising all my time and not just company time, when I'm in an office, a site, or one of the company's many facilities.

It's just too difficult for me to open my laptop in this tiny seat. Each time I try, the people on either side of me want to move, or the person in front of me wants to recline his chair. Despite this, I eventually start to appreciate my seat. The inability to unpack my laptop has caused me to relax and even watch a movie. It has also forced me to use a pen and paper and write notes. This is how I started building my book of thoughts in the first place, so happily, I keep on scribbling. I guess now I need to thank my company for its new travel rule, as I actually used the flight time to relax, watch a movie, and scribble notes, where I would have normally been working. So what I initially posed as a negative turned out to be a positive. As I often say, if you think positive, most times the outcome will be positive.

But – and yes, I keep repeating this incredible three-letter word – what has any of that got to do with the title of this chapter, 'The Way to Heaven'? Nothing, I guess, unless you think there are rules and things we must adhere to, to get to heaven. What do you think? Are there rules and conditions set by God for us to get into Heaven?

I'm not sure if you've used this time to write something in the space above. Perhaps you thought it was a silly question to begin with, as your beliefs have already conditioned you to know how to get into heaven. On the other hand, do you fall into another group, which never gave it much thought and doesn't see why to think about it now?

Maybe that's why I write, as thinking is a major part of my life. I also love posing questions that may not have a detailed answer or answers that are not founded on facts but more on beliefs and conditioning, using evidence gained from the existing thoughts of people who have been empowered to influence the masses.

Never repeat what others have said but first find out for yourself, test it out yourself, testing what you think, what you see, not test what others have said:

—J. Krishnamurti

I enjoy exploring my own ability to logically answer questions raised on most subjects. I say 'most' as I believe I do not need to know all the answers, nor do I need to raise a question on all things, even when the answers are not easy to understand or explain. However, I am always interested in other people's opinions and thoughts. My aim is not to challenge them or to challenge my own belief but simply to seek other views. As I have an open mind, it is good for me and hopefully others to explore how other individuals think.

This is especially true when the answer or belief is well-known, as I am intrigued to listen to how some people easily explain without justification and others will seek consensus, which could be seen as questionable in relation to what they think or believe. Remember, I'm only offering a single opinion, and the question I am raising now and thinking about is how one may get into heaven. It must also be said that I am having this thought while being bounced around due to weather conditions and heavy turbulence. I am continually hearing the sounds of others taking deep sighs and exclaiming, 'Ah!' and 'Oh!' as we are all strapped in a smaller-than-small seat due to new company rules.

Sorry, I think I was complaining. Of course, they are my company rules and not those of the hundreds of other passengers on the plane, who are happy just having a seat. But maybe not today, due to bad weather and turbulence Still, let's look on the bright side. I am not six feet six inches tall, and I haven't eaten my way to obesity yet, so I try my best to focus, think and look around. I allow my eyes to drift and look outside to a wing that is moving up and down, which leads me to have an intriguing thought. What if this turns out to be my final trip?

I imagine thinking, *OK, this is my last few minutes on this Earth, and the airplane is out of control!* Our chances of survival are next to none. What do I do? Do I scream and get into the crash position? Coincidentally, I think the crash position is pointless. A good position, I feel, is one that you are in. I would say to find a position that you feel relaxed in. However, I do not think anyone (unless they are unconscious) would be relaxed as the plane is being torn apart and there's panic and terror all around you from fellow passengers. This is especially true since the odds of surviving a plane crash in bad weather and over water are limited. I thought about calling the stewardess and offering my recommendation of putting on a comedy and letting us all laugh as we go down. Now, I'm not being morbid. But as I am now fifty-five years old and I travel more than the average person, it could be argued that I belong in a high-risk group and am closer to my final adventure than others who may be reading this chapter.

Furthermore, over the past few months, I have had a few friends pass away. Others have been diagnosed with some not-so-nice diseases that will take them from this Earth, in my opinion, well before their time – whatever that may mean, as there is never a good time to die. We still shed tears and feel sorrow if a person who has died was young or very old. I think everyone has a 'use-by date,' like a hidden barcode. We all believe that we shall live until we are old, especially as the mortality rates are increasing. So in most cases, when death comes, we and our family and friends are not prepared to die. But death is not prejudiced. It comes to us all, without any consideration of age, gender, or nationality.

I shall emphasise here that while I offer my opinion of that mystical myth of how someone can get to heaven, I have no evidence of such a place personally. I did attend Bible classes and have read lots on different religious groups and their beliefs. I've even engaged in debates with others who say that their religion is most in touch with

God, whatever that may mean. I do not think you get a direct pass to heaven just because you're linked with a certain group or religion. This is something that is personal and within us all, as it is our own belief, not the beliefs of others. However, no one has actually said they have been to Heaven, apart from a few drunks and others who were high on something you couldn't buy over the counter.

I shall not be able to say here what or where heaven is. I can only rely on my own personal views, opinions, and knowledge; I have not been able to discuss the matter with anyone who has been there. Heaven isn't like a holiday destination, where you can log on to heavenlytravel.com and book your final trip. You can't discuss details of your final trip with an angel at the heavenly travel desk and ask for info on the deals that they have, so you can plan ahead and even save a little time. Sorry, no discounts are given. It's a one-way ticket, with no guarantee that we will even get there. As far as I know, you're not allowed any carry-on luggage on the next phase of your journey. But maybe there are other things that we need to do while living.

Do ordinary things with extraordinary love.

—Mother Teresa

I, personally, have established a global internal well-being savings account structured for me and only for me. It's an account that doesn't offer any financial rewards. It is left to me to manage it and make deposits as I wish and feel is appropriate. I have named this my legacy to mankind, or me-kind, as I am talking about myself and how I choose to live my life while I'm alive. This means I do my best every day to be kind, share thoughts, and offer a kind word or a few coins. I look after my direct family and where possible friends and others in need, with the aim of giving a little every day to others without being asked or expecting anything in return. I do this because I can and want to, not because I believe this shall be considered a down payment or an entry fee into heaven.

We should all live the life we wish to live and not consider what is beyond this life, as living in the future is taking us away from the present. My global well-being savings account is about me enjoying myself, at that time and place and with whoever I may be with. This allows me to share my smile, laughter, and knowledge and whatever I feel is appropriate and needed. I repeat, this is me being me and enjoying the moment while trying to do my best. I truly believe you cannot build credits in this life for the next, so it does amaze me how some people, as they get older or become sick, find religion or return to their faith. Please don't get me wrong; it is up to the individual to do so. If that makes the final periods of life easier to accept, then that is excellent. But how can anyone think that they can dial God and ask for forgiveness? Firstly, who has the number? Plus, in my mind and thought pattern, by then it is too late. Whatever has been done has been done, and only you know why it was done. So I say, don't ask for forgiveness until you understand what you are asking forgiveness for. Then swear to yourself it will never happen again. If your deed involved another, pray that he or she will forgive you, as that is the most beautiful and powerful gift any person can give.

However, before I go any further, I shall say with all sincerity that I don't write my opinions to offend. If for whatever reason someone finds my words upsetting or offensive, I offer the following things. Firstly, I apologise, not because I did anything wrong but because my written words have caused you to think and one of those thoughts may have been that I have done wrong. Secondly, I shall advise you not to read any more. Turn to another chapter, as I shall explore my own views of heaven in more detail later within this chapter. And lastly, buy another book that leaves you feeling happy and content because it gives you the words and ending that you wish for.

In life we are not guaranteed anything, apart from paying tax, which can vary depending on who you are and where you live. It is a depressing prospect, to give our money to governments and individuals within governments who struggle to manage their own household's budget. What a cynical thought? Yes, especially when we look across the world and see what all governments do: procrastinate on decision making with the aim of being re-elected. This is done to try and create harmony and trust across all the people of the country, which is basically impossible. There will always be differences, which will put greater pressure on a government that tries to please a certain group over others. However, this is not just a government problem. This is a voters' problem too, as we live in a world where we expect fast and quick solutions.

As the population grows and communications improve, governments can no longer hide their mistakes. What we, the people of the world, should understand is that we cannot always have our own way. Changes can take time. Some changes shall be hard to digest initially, and governments must have strong leaders with administrations that are efficient and effective. However, this is what most people don't like: a government that is disciplined.

The world is not only hungry for food but also beauty

—Mother Teresa

However, I have digressed, so back to the future – or the end, depending on how you view this final journey. We must all face the 100 per cent guaranteed final journey. In my opinion, the final step is the one step where we are all equals. When the lights go out, they leave all those materialistic things behind, including all that you may own and all the money you have saved over time. Now they will do you no good. They will stay where you last saw them, before the light went out and you took your final breath. There is no transfer of belongings where we will end up, and this is a fact. It does not matter what you believe. But of course, some may choose to have a beautiful send-off, spending huge amounts of money on the funeral, service, memorial, interment, burial, cremation, rites, and procession, not forgetting the wake.

At the wake, all we really do is drink and eat. Some may get drunk while reminiscing of times gone by. If I am to be honest, I am sure spending lots of money on a fancy box. The ceremony is just a means for some to show off their wealth for the last time. Having a flashy funeral, or whatever you may wish to call it, is money not well spent, I think, as your box will either be buried or burnt. Either way, in the majority of cases, the box is never seen again after you are put to rest. I like that term, 'rest.' We have all read those cards or obituaries ending with 'RIP,' or 'rest in peace'. When we leave this Earth, we also leave all our worries, pain, and suffering behind. There is no greater rest than your final rest. There will be no alarm calls or rush hour traffic, just the purest of rest. Whatever happens on this Earth after we leave, we shall never see, hear, or experience it, or have to worry about it, as we are gone.

I am sure some may disagree and say that bad people or people of different beliefs shall be damned and transported to Hell. But then again, I haven't met anyone who has been to Hell in the way some religious groups may portray it. However, I have met many people who have lived in Hell while living on this Earth. None of them have said that they met any fellows with horns sticking out of their heads, as Satan is often described, or been made to shovel coal to keep the fire of damnation alight and burning. I may sound flippant, but in my opinion, God is too good and loving to punish anyone.

Therefore, I totally disagree with any religious belief that states nonbelievers, or people of different beliefs, shall rot in hell. 'Rot' is an interesting word. We can talk more about that later.

I do think, however, that some people do experience a living Hell while alive. But as I said before, these are man-made things, not God-made things. That include but not limited to: "hatred, greed, jealousy, discrimination, prejudice, bigotry War, abuse, and greed". So I repeat, I don't believe in Hell after this life. But as I have written before, we may have a couple of options. One is that we die, stay dead, and rot away after being buried or cremated. The other is that we transcend into Heaven. Whichever it may be, you will not know until it happens, which means you have left your body and this life.

I would just like to say here that I won't mind if people want to hold a wake or even a party in celebration of my life, as I would like people to remember me, for all the good and the bad, and say their good-byes in a single day. Thereafter, they may remember me for what I did or did not do and the things I have achieved or not achieved. As I will not be there, they should say and feel as they wish, as whatever is said cannot hurt me but may help the people whom I have left behind to move forward and live their lives. To those I leave behind, I'd like to say again, it is your life, and you should never live in the shoes of another. Those shoes may not fit, and your feet may become sore.

Leaving this life and all the things they own may sadden some, so I guess that's why some very rich (and in my opinion strange) people have paid large amounts of money to have their bodies frozen via 'cryopreservation.' Basically, your body is put in cold storage with the hope of being resurrected in years to come. However, this depends on future advancements in repair technologies. Cryonics is still hypothetical and has yet to be proven. But who am I to say it will not work? Let them have their final wishes. If it comes true and they are returned to life, what will they come back to? A new world? A new life? And what memories would they have, if any, of their old life? But again, let's amuse ourselves. I believe the people who will be reading this book will not consider placing their already dead bodies into a freezer. Whoops! Sorry, I mean taking up the option of cryopreservation, which I might add, if I have read correctly, has to be done very quickly after death. So the next time you are travelling, please ensure your insurance covers a deep freezer truck with the ability to snap freeze you wherever you may be. Sorry … again, my cynicism is showing.

I may be wrong, as I have been wrong before. After all, I'm human, and humans make mistakes. So for the sake of completing this paragraph, let's say they do return in future years. They may then realise they are alone, wrinkly, and old as well as lost in time, as things will have changed. Maybe as so many years have passed, future generations will put them on show as the twenty-first-century specimen of the human form. Maybe they will feed them and care for them, but keep them locked away to perform for our futuristic brothers and sisters. So let just hope the owners of these cryonic facilities remember to pay their electricity bills in advance and the laws of the land don't change.

Otherwise, those frozen corpses may be removed and sent into space, along with all of the earth's waste that can't be stored due to centuries of not understanding the important of preserving our environment. Or am I hoping for too much? By the time these frozen relics of time past are defrosted, they may be shocked to find people living in isolated units away from natural air, having caused so much pollution that nature is uninhabitable and we no longer trust anything other than test tube products.

Whoops, sorry, I'm showing a little bit of silliness. In simple terms, getting back to the couple of hundred people that have been frozen – if they returned and none of the above happened, it still would not be the life they left behind. That life was lost, and I would say the majority of people that they knew in the past would either have died or be very old and close to dying. Having been resurrected, would such people live alone, trying to understand who they were in the past and why they really wanted to return? I am not convinced that cryonics will ever work, but man was never meant to fly or go into space, so what do I know? I know I do not think this is an option I would like, even if it did work.

I think maybe the best option is to take the final step with dignity, if possible, take your chances, and hope we are all allowed to transcend into the next life. There, we may meet loved ones and others whom we have never met. We shall forever be blessed to sit in the company of free-spirited spirits. Now. I'm not referring to hundred-year-old scotch or any other alcoholic beverage. I am talking about the beautiful celestial place where we no longer seek self-gratification, go to war, feel hatred or envy, or discriminate against others. Instead, we float in a mystical place that removes any needs and wants, as we are all finally equal, being unable to see or feel differences.

This will be your final resting place, and if you wish to call it Heaven, please do so. Forever believe and never lose your faith, as this will help you accept that final journey without fear of death. My greatest fear is that when that day comes, I shall leave this Earth without dignity, and the people I leave will mourn my death instead of celebrating my life.

I will gladly accept the tears of the people who have known me or taken the time to come and say their final good-byes either at my wake or the funeral service, as these people liked me and loved me as I was. However, I want them to continue to live their lives and not feel sorrow for my passing. If I appear in their minds as a memory of times past, I hope they have nice thoughts, and if they cry, that's OK. Crying is a natural part of mourning, but I want them to know and understand that I have gone. They need not worry about where I have gone to. All they need to think is, I lived, loved, and lived some more; I will forever be with them in their hearts, minds, and thoughts; and I will forever love them as they were.

I hope my family and friends will think of me and talk about me occasionally, but I ask that they accept that I am now at rest and in peace. I truly believe that we shall all be at peace at the end of this life. But I shall live on forever, in the memories of those who loved me and talk about me, until they take that final journey and rest in peace.

Old friends pass away, new friends appear. It is just like the days. An old day passes, a new day arrives. The important thing is to make it meaningful: a meaningful friend – or a meaningful day.

—**Dalai Lama**

I woke up this morning with a burning thought about judgement day. Are you ready? I am about to enlighten you. You see, it is my belief that every day in which we are alive and walking this Earth is judgement day. That's why, years ago, I opened my global internal well-being savings account. We do not want to leave this world with any regrets, and I am sure you will not be surprised when I say that as I close my eyes for the very last time, I do not believe I shall be attacked by whirling black shadows that will usher me to door 666, for my placement interview with the devil's clan. Or do I think I shall be greeted with whiter-than-white lights and sent floating into the heavenly sky, to be dropped off at the pearly gates of Heaven to meet God, where we shall discuss the meaning of Heaven or even what beautiful weather it is today – sorry, that day?

That decision shall already be made. We shall all be at rest and no longer walking this Earth in the physical sense. We will be here in the memories of those people that we have touched, loved, and respected, as we have deposited some good wishes, a few coins, or even a smile. Whatever we have done in our life shall be the final judgement and your judgement. No one else shall be able to judge you. That's why we should always show respect and live the life we choose, using our time with others as if it will be our last. Show respect, kindness, and love.

Be kind whenever possible. It is always possible.

—**Dalai Lama**

CHAPTER 8

Whatever

Whatever. What a wonderful word. It often leaves the receiver of the message with a bewildered feeling. Whether we like to accept 'whatever' or not as a reply, I think it's a great way to start a new chapter after chapter 7, which said lots but also said it without saying 'whatever'.

What matters is what you think, how you live. And to find out how you live, how you act, what you do, you have to discard totally all knowledge of the experts and professionals who have instructed you how to live:

—J. Krishnamurti

Well, I could say 'whatever' after that quotation, but what I shall say instead is my interpretation of the quotation. I think it is saying that being yourself means you need to gain intellectual and individual freedom, and that is the beauty of being human. In simple terms, to be aware of all things is impossible, so to accept being unaware is the way to go. Life needs to be lived until we die. We must always approach all things in a state of not knowing and accept the surprises that come with it. That is an interesting concept: 'accept the surprise'. It is great in theory but much easier to write than actually do. It will depend on the surprise, of course, as some surprises are hard to take and so unacceptable we may need to run, hide, or put our heads in the sand and hope they will go away. Have you ever watched a child play hide and seek? Their innocence allows them to believe that if they cannot see you, you cannot see them.

However, as adults, we know that doing nothing or closing our eyes to the outside world will not protect us from 'whatever.' Many surprises come without any announcement, as that is what makes a surprise a surprise. Therefore, we should accept we do not know all that may occur, remembering we can ask questions if we feel we need to know or want to know. Otherwise, we can ask nothing and accept whatever comes, good or bad.

Knowing is the thirst of the young and the desire of the old, but no one knows everything. Therefore, how can there be truth? What I know or what I hear may be different from what you know. I would say that if we continually accept the thoughts and lectures of others without truly analysing and challenging them, our knowledge base is limited.

In my opinion, we often allow ourselves to be imprisoned by the words, thoughts, and conditioning of others. Clearly, this is not being an independent thinker, as independence means listening, learning, and then deciding and making choices. Collecting data without considering the worth of those data is turning your mind into a wasteland, as personal knowledge that is unshared is, in my view, not intelligence but isolation and madness.

Knowledge has to be gained, and not just from books or the thoughts and lectures of others. Step outside your own mind and look in as a third person. Continually challenge your own beliefs and feelings based on all that you know, which has been gained through life experiences, experiments, and making mistakes. Gurus, experts, professors, and all those authors of self-help books may offer us advice and lecture us on how we should live our lives. However, they rarely share experiments that went wrong or describe how their brilliant findings came from making a mistake.

What is true and magical is the unlimited insight of seeing something as it is.

What is an opinion? Is it everything you see and hear that's truthful?

Ploughing a field without seeding it is just turning over the soil. Where in the end, the soil will be so ploughed and fine it will blow away – is this an original thought? Not sure but I did write it.

As I write, something dawns upon me. Could it be that no thought is totally independent and original? The future is not in your thoughts, as knowledge is no more than what is known and never the unknown. But to confuse you, I shall now disagree with the above view, as thoughts are not always limited if they are challenged. Thoughts arise from the process of organising and un-organising functional and dysfunctional knowledge gained not solely through our conditioning but also through our senses. This, in my opinion, is one of the purest ways of gaining knowledge, as an individual captures those distinct and special moments where we absorb all that is being sent out to be retrieved through our 5 + 1 = 6 senses: sight, hearing, touch, smell, taste, and (as I always say) brain.

Looking to the sky, you may be amazed at how fresh and blue it appears, without a cloud in sight. Then you look again. Clouds start rolling in independently, but with such grace that they appear to have been carefully ushered in, like a dance composition to the music of the wind. All around, solo performances are occurring with nature. All living things, including the trees, plants, birds, and others, come alive in harmonistic movements. The trees sway, and leaves fall floating to the ground. Birds fly and dive, while passers-by hold on to coats. This is now, here and new. This is both beautiful and magical. as it highlights the beauty that is all around and is free to experience.

Young children's minds and thoughts are wonderful, as they are not yet corrupted and totally conditioned. This is evident in how they can spend hours playing with next to nothing, or create imaginary friends, or how they can watch insects with their mouths and eyes fully open, taking in every little moment. I've written before that a child may take forever to walk just ten metres. They are using all of their senses, capturing everything around them. We adults, on the other hand, move with such haste that we only capture bits and pieces. This is because we are on a different journey, an adult journey, which believes that stopping and smelling the roses is a waste of time. People are so conditioned. We have become creatures of habit and routine, so much so that to allow our minds and thoughts freedom or some quality time may be against our beliefs, values, and conditioning. Please listen and understand that you should look for quality in your life, not quantity. Rushing from place to place or book to book does not allow us the time we need to connect 100 per cent with all that is around us, so that we may be free to see, hear, touch, taste, and feel.

Some may look at me as being eccentric or a little mad. As I stand and watch, fascinated by the richness of colours and freshness of a windy day, I see, hear, and become part of nature's dance.

On a rainy day, I walk more slowly, allowing nature's tears to become my tears as my clothes and skin become soaked. This simple act makes me feel rejuvenated. I am now one with the Earth and all living things. In this moment, I am no longer accepting those words or instructions from years past that form my thoughts, such as 'Do not get wet or you shall get a cold.' Now I hear myself say, 'Whatever.' I am drenched due to the constant rain that's coming from all angles, and I'm caught in gusts of wind that swirl around me, creating sounds that continually change. I am one of the wind's instruments, as the wind uses both solid and not-so-solid structures as instruments to blow and beat in order to create its musical masterpiece.

For the man sound of body and serene of mind there is no such thing as bad weather; every day has its beauty, and storms which whip the blood do but make it pulse more vigorously.

—George Gissing

Our senses are how we gain personal information that is there to take. However, one must understand all the information that our senses are sending to our brain. This information needs interpreting for it to be transmitted, understood, and remembered. All the data being collected must first be stored and encoded.

I am not going to try to explain here the different systems or the complexity of the brain, as I do not know it in its entirety, nor do others. The scientific world continually explores the brain through research, so my limited knowledge on the matter would not give the answers that you, the reader, may want. I will say, however, that even the best of the best scientists who are considered the experts in this field and spend millions of dollars and hours on research are still struggling to fully understand how our brains works, particularly in storing information and then encoding it.

Maybe that's why, in the name of science, Albert Einstein's brain was removed within eight hours of his death. It has been reported that after being weighed, photographed, and tested by leading physicians of that time (1955), it was then dissected into pieces.

The numbers of pieces vary depending on what book you read, but a number that jumps into my mind is 240. Again, I cannot be certain of the number or how small these pieces were, but what I do know is that it happened. I can appreciate the quest to find out the inner workings of a mechanical instrument, machine, or something that has broken down. We can, after all, take it apart and then put it back together. But did those people who studied the small sections of Einstein's brain truly believe that they would be able to decode how his brain worked and, moreover, how he thought?

We know from all the material on Einstein, including biographies of his life, that he thought outside the box. He also continually challenged the establishment and rules. I am sure this could not have been seen in those small, dissected pieces, which were sent off to be reviewed, analysed, and whatever. However, I must conclude by saying that if you want to further study this topic, there has been much written about Einstein for you to enjoy. Studies have identified that parts of his brain were different from other men's. Sadly, this was identified from analysing photos of his whole brain, not the smaller than small pieces.

In our haste to find out his brilliance we may have destroyed more than we shall ever know. If only the physician had the foresight and patience to preserve his brain, this would have enabled future generations with advanced technology to analyse the real thing instead of looking at photos.

However, so as not to bore you or to get the 'whatever' response from you, the reader, I shall say that sometimes the information that our senses pick up for our brain to encode could be misinterpreted. This is because the brain may not totally understand the signals we are sending, as it depends on the numbers of senses in use and what is being transmitted to the brain. Is the signal clear or unclear?

We humans, especially older humans, have lived and experienced so much that we do not want to hear our brains saying, 'I am confused.'

That would send the echoes of thousands of voices through the millions of cells, nerves, and complex systems within the brain. Each part of the body would then communicate with the others through a human superhighway that controls every part of your daily life, from breathing to blinking, walking, and sleeping. These parts themselves never sleep. The human highway gives us our memories, which are formed from our exposure to the facts and experiences we collect every moment we are alive. Nerves reach from your brain to your face, ears, eyes, nose, and spinal cord. Each and every part of you is connected and wired.

Here is a trivial bit of information that you may not know. In one square inch of skin, there are four yards of nerve fibres, six hundred pain sensors, 1,300 nerve cells, nine thousand nerve endings, thirty-six heat sensors, seventy-five pressure sensors, a hundred sweat glands, three million cells, and three yards of blood vessels (http://vinodpaulson. hubpages.com/hub/AMAZING_HUMAN_FACTS).

The some page states, 'our brain is more complex than the most powerful computer and has over a hundred billion nerve cells.' I shall not argue with this, as I do not know how many nerve cells there are in the brain. What I know is, my brain gives me the power to make a decision based on information stored and held within memory systems that have been gained through experiences, knowledge, beliefs, and conditioning. All this happens in nanoseconds or less, so we have a clear image, smell, or feeling of what we are sensing. This is brilliant, but is it real or the truth? Can it be trusted? Are our minds and thoughts free to interpret without any prejudice, or are our thoughts blocked by our perceptions, which are continually being enforced by our conditioning, beliefs, and values?

Only one who devotes himself to a cause with his whole strength and soul can be a true master. For this reason mastery demands all of a person.

—Albert Einstein

Sometimes, I feel it is important to self-evaluate or decondition yourself, whatever we may call it. I treat this as my wake-up period, as I do not want to slip into the zombie zone where I drift without thought or meaning. I am human, an individual, and I have a brain. I want it to work and give me positive thoughts so that my state of mind is one of quality and not just one that is just accepting the known and not considering the unknown.

I do not want to be prejudiced, racist, discriminatory, or unkind. I want a mind that is free of these beliefs. But for me and others to gain a state of mind that is free, we must understand how we are driven to hating one another due to differences in beliefs, culture, language, race and colour.

Are we conditioned to accept or not accept? Do my beliefs and values influence my behaviours? I would say yes, and it is those that we need to review, evaluate, and every now and then decondition. If we don't do this, we shall never feel freedom of thought as we did when we were young. In our youth – or I should say in my youth, as I do not want to assume anything – we constantly searched and inquired to fulfil the voids or perceived voids within us. Our emotional state changed as our age and experiences grew. Most of us drift through these wonderful times, too busy trying to take the next step to understand the journey we are on. However, due to our conditioning, this can be frustrating as we continually struggle to appease others. We do this while looking for our road in life, not knowing or accepting that we may never find it or that we may have found it, but our desire to please others made us move on.

Being in my fifties, I can say that those early years were great, even with all the heartache and abuse. They were some of the most confusing, tormenting, but overall beautiful journeys of my life. However, as we move from adolescence to being older, many become more settled with our day-to-day routines. Those routines become habits, and we feel safe. Our extraordinary zest for life disappears, and we become respectable, petty, and thoughtless.

As our mind stops challenging the unknown and we accept our perception of life as right, we begin to argue, fight, and become racist, discriminatory, and hateful. This chapter is titled 'Whatever,' but I dislike words that can cause pain, such as 'fat', 'hate', 'ugly', and 'stupid'. These words can stick. I wish I could say 'whatever', but when I hear them being said, especially to others, they bother me too.

I need music, as the last few paragraphs are taking me down the road of realism. Here, even my positive mind and thoughts are struggling to appear. Then the sounds of Al Jarreau start to fill my body, so I close my eyes to think of love. 'Love is all around' is one of my favourite lines, from one of my favourite movies, *Love Actually*. The next time you are out, look with an open mind. You will be amazed at how much love you will see. Witness the love of a mother, father, brother, or sister and the love of a stranger that puts a few coins in the hand of a person in need. Love is all around, but so is hatred.

Do you hate?

I could not let any of my chapters, within any one of my books, finish with the thought of hatred without giving my view of that horrible word and concept. I hear people say, 'I hate that place!' It could be food, a thing, or a person. This strong emotional feeling drives our dislikes. I say, do not hate. Dislike if you want, but we should be trying to remove hatred from our minds. Otherwise, we shall never be able to live in peace.

While civilization has been improving our houses, it has not equally improved the men who are to inhabit them. It has created palaces, but it was not so easy to create noblemen and kings.

—Henry David Thoreau

'Whatever', you may say. I shall write the following letters, L-O-V-E, and ask you read the lyrics from Nat King Cole's song: 'L-O-V-E'

To close this chapter, let us repeat what I wrote at the beginning 'Whatever' – what a wonderful word. It leaves the receiver of the message bewildered. Whether we like to accept it or not, 'whatever' marks the end to chapter 7, which said lots, but also said it without saying 'whatever.'

CHAPTER 9

All in a Name, Random Thoughts, and Silliness

First you forget names, then you forget faces. Next you forget to pull your zipper up, and finally, you forget to pull it down.

—George Burns

How protective are you of your name? I mean, for years, I have heard people say, 'No, my name is...' and, 'No, you pronounce it this way ...' Therefore, I think I'm pretty lucky, as my name is quite common and easy to pronounce.

'John', I've been told, means 'Gracious'. *Why gracious?* I thought, as a name is just a name. It's a means to call someone. In Australia we call people 'mate', which is fine. But a room of unknown people being called 'mate' could get confusing, unless you numbered them mates one, two, three, and so on. Now I understand in a childish way that names were invented to make us more recognisable. So to suppress my curiosity, a-researching I went. I was to find out that the name 'John' is masculine and is actually pronounced 'Jahn'. The name apparently came from the English form of Iohannes, from the Latin form of the Greek name Ioannes, which in itself is derived from the Hebrew name Yochanan, meaning 'YAHWEH is gracious'. Still, I wondered, why is my name so common? For instance, my mother was married to three

Johns, not at the same time, but that's another story. As I continue to read about the origins of my name, I am informed that the name 'John' owes its popularity to two New Testament characters, the first being John the Baptist and the second the apostle John.

The name John (in various spellings) has been borne by twenty-one popes and eight devious emperors as well as rulers of England, France, Sweden, Denmark, Poland, Portugal, Bulgaria, Russia, and Hungary. It was also borne by the poet John Milton (1608–1674), the philosopher John Locke (1632–1704), the American founding father and president John Adams (1735–1826), and the poet John Keats (1795–1821).

However, what about more modern times, such as the twentieth century? We have author John Steinbeck (1902–1968), assassinated American president John F. Kennedy (1917–1963), and musician John Lennon (1940–1980). All this useful information, by the way, was found on the following website: www.behindthename.com.

However, let's have a reality check. To prove that my ego hasn't swollen to ridiculous proportions after reading the above, I shall also say that if I were travelling through America, I would never respond to, 'Where is the John?' when it is being called out. That means someone is looking for a toilet, and even if my pockets are large, they are not to be used by some larger-than-large Yank (whoops! American fellow) to offload his swollen bladder!

However, let's explore my surname, 'Christian', which is another easy name to remember but again could receive raised eyebrows because of religious thoughts. I'm pleased I live in the twenty-first century and not the Roman days, as I may have had to fight a lion or two. However, from the same web page, I found that it derives from the Medieval Latin name Christianus, meaning 'a Christian'. Ah, lions are getting hungry just from the very mention of my surname! That's why I'm pleased as heck that I was born in 1958, when being fed to lions was no longer fashionable. However, my name has been used in England since the Middle Ages, during which time it was used by both males and females. Still, the name did not become common until the seventeenth century. In Denmark, the name has been borne by ten kings since the fifteenth century. A famous bearer was Hans Christian Andersen (1805–1875), the Danish author of such fairy tales as 'The Ugly Duckling' and 'The Emperor's New Clothes'.

Now, I am impressed, as I love those stories and the author. Once, when I was in the Royal Air Force, I was given the nickname 'Hans Christian Anderson'. Why? Well, I was leading a group of recruits in an exercise. The corporal set the scene, describing the scenario and how a green field was a raging river. I thought for a moment and then went into action, deploying my vehicles and carrying out the rescue mission. However, at the debrief, the corporal said I had failed, as all my men had died in the river. My response was simple. I said, 'Corporal, if you see the raging river on a flat bit of green ground, surely you can also see the four-lane bridge that I built to transport my vehicles across the raging river!' His response was, 'We'd better start calling you Hans Christian Anderson from now on!' I passed the exercise with good marks, and from that day on, I became a storyteller ... but not to the same level as Hans Christian Anderson.

Then, after moving to Australia when I was twenty-three and had left the armed services, I was given the names 'Johnno', 'John the Pom', and in later years 'JC', which again all have a meaning. 'Johnno' came about because Australians have this habit of lengthening a name by adding on an 'o.' Why? Well, I'm not sure, but did it offend me? No. 'John the Pom' was coined to let me and others know that I was not an Australian native. You see, 'Pom' means 'Prisoner of Her Majesty'! I can say with all honesty that this isn't true, as I have never stolen a loaf of bread, nor was I ever charged with an offence against Her Majesty that would have had me banished to Australia.

I immigrated to Australia in 1981 from the UK, and paid my own way arriving with six hundred pound sterling in my pocket, so technically I cannot be called a Pom, as my passage was not free or exciting as I was mot banished for crimes against Her Majesty It would have been a lot cheaper and maybe even more exciting than our DC10 airplane trip, which at the time was having problems with engineers, the door flying off, and an array of other incidents that had made the aviation master ground the plane. But that's another story, which has been written about, researched, and used, I am sure, to capture the imagination of movie producers across the world. To shed some light on Australian history, the last prisoner was sent to Australia in 1868, so my arrival in 1981 was some 113 years too late.

How time flies! In those early years, we worked hard, and one year turned into the next. After living in Australia for three years, I was given one of the greatest gifts that any man could receive – the birth of my daughter, Claire.

Pictures were sent and phone calls were made to family, especially the ever-doting grandparents who were still living in England. Then we received even more calls, demanding, 'When will we see her?' As my jetlag and fear of flying had finally worn off, we packed our bags and travelled back to England to show our beautiful girl. Some three and half years had passed, and on my return, I thought I would go and have a pint of beer in the Crown, a local pub that had been sold to a person called Henry Christian for eight guineas around 1770. Note: 'The guinea was a British coin until 1779. In fact it was the first British machine-struck gold coin and had a value of one pound. However, the name continued in use to reflect approximately twenty-one shillings = one pound and one shilling.'

I remember the name and sum of money paid, as there was a plaque on the wall declaring this. I often wondered if Henry Christian and I were related. However, I never investigated it, nor did I actually look deeply into my family tree. I thought, generally, that we the Christian family were dysfunctional, but back to the story. As I sat drinking my brown and mild, an old local came over and said, 'Hi young fellow! I have not seen you for a while,' to which I replied, 'I have been away for three and a half years.'

'Ah,' he said, 'You must have been a bad bugger!'

'No!' I replied. 'I've been to Australia!'

He looked shocked and walked away in silence. Did he think England was still sending people to Australia for committing crimes? Well, it made me smile.

My final nickname is 'JC', which is simply the initials of my first and last names. But quite often, it gets linked to the name that Christian believers would think of – Jesus Christ. Believe me, over all the years that I was called JC, none of the people calling me that were thinking of me in any religious context. However, thinking of my construction days, the name 'Jesus Christ' was used frequently, and again not in a religious context. It was said when someone was in pain or frustrated. For example, when someone hit their finger with a hammer, they would typically shout out, 'Oh Jesus Christ!' I'm not sure why or who started it. Perhaps it was a priest shouting for help, or an atheist looking for belief and salvation. Who knows?

So does my name have any special connection to anything for me? Not really; it's just my name. My first name came about perhaps due to my mother not having much imagination or just liking the name John, as she was actually married to three of them that I know of. I believe there may have been another, which would have made it four. My surname came from my father, whom I've never really met, so does that have any true meaning? Not really, apart from reminding me that I did not have a father in my life – well, a biological father anyway – who wanted to stay. So call me whatever you wish, as long as you don't call me late for dinner!

However, if I were to choose another name for my own, like so many movie stars, what would I call myself? Perhaps 'Everlasting Spring'? Or 'Moonlight'? Or another strange moniker? The answer is no. I am happy with the name I was given, even if it is quite common and even though my surname could have gotten me stoned or fed to the lions at one point in history, or even now if I were to venture to the war-torn sections of the Middle East. My name is John and it is mine, and I was given it by my mother. As all boys know, they should never argue with their mothers!

I remember a trip to Paris in 2013 that got me a new first and last name, which I thought was quite amusing. As I checked into the Meridian Hotel, I said to the beautiful receptionist in my impressively poor spoken French, 'Hello, m'y réservation is under thé name Christian,' which in English sounds the same without my bad French accent. Instantly realising that my French was poorer than that of the poorest French speaker on this Earth, she replied in a most charming and sophisticated tone, 'Would you like me to speak English?'

As I spoke, I tried to make my voice sound less like a cat being skinned alive. As my friends have told me, my voice and accent sound a lot like a concrete mixer with broken cogs on steroids, and to make it worse, all this is in turbo, as I tend to speak very fast. While overseas, in countries where the first language isn't English, I do my very best to speak slower than the slowest of tortoises, which would never really have won the race against the hare. That, I think, was a story made up by a frustrated but slow runner.

Anyway, let's get back to the check-in. The receptionist then said, 'Sorry, sir, we have no reservations for a person called Mr Christian.' The blood drained from my face, but as the receptionist was smiling, I stayed calm. Then she asked for my first name, to which I replied, 'John, as written on my passport.' She looked at her computer in great detail. After a few more minutes of looking, she announced that she had found a reservation for an Australian with the surname of 'Jahnchristsen', with a first name of 'Mr'. That amused me, so I replied, 'That's me!' Without looking up, she then asked how she should address me. Or was it 'undress me?' Sorry, my mind slipped into the gutter for a second there. Remember, in America John does mean toilet! So I repeat, she said, 'How should I address you?'

'By my fist name,' I replied. She said, 'OK,' and called me 'Mr', which made us both laugh. But then she called me 'Mr John', as I'm sure trying to pronounce 'Mr Jahnchristsen' would have been hard for anyone.

I really can't see why any of us should get upset or offended when our names our pronounced incorrectly. It's only a name. But then, I do recall another time when I was at Catterick, North Yorkshire, while I was in the armed services. This time, my name was pronounced100 per cent correctly, but I wish it had been mispronounced! This person asked, 'Is there a person called John Christian in the bar?' To which I replied, 'Yes!' Unfortunately, this earned me a punch in the face! Why I was punched is another story, and it has nothing to do with either my first or last names.

Lesson learnt: When someone calls out your name and you don't know them, I would suggest you ask first what they want from that person, before jumping up and saying, 'That's me!' Otherwise you may receive a surprise punch on the nose.

Forgive your enemies, but never forget their names.

—**John F. Kennedy**

What is the meaning of your name?

First Name:
Surname:

Are you happy with your name, or would you like to change it?

Do you think it is important for a woman to take her husband's family name?

My personal answer to that last one is, it should be a woman's choice, not the choice of the man or some old-fashioned law that ties a woman to her man like a slave to her master. I am sure my opinion is not that of many others, and you may have a totally different view on this. A name, to me, is only important so that we know what to call someone when we need to talk, communicate, or even buy them dinner.

However, when saying that, I do wonder how parents come up with names for their children. Some cultures believe that the name is important, as each name has a special meaning. Then again, some people insist on giving their children very unusual names. Yes, at the time it may seem like a nice, appropriate name. But don't these parents consider the later years? What if they named their child after their favourite football team, or gave them some peace-loving hippy moniker like 'Living-Pain' or 'Rosechild'? My name came about due to lack of imagination and following a tradition. It could have been worse. While travelling in the States, I was amazed at how many children have their father's names, ending with 'Junior' or a number. Just think, I could have been called 'Christian the third', or 'John Robert Christian Junior'. This is the question I pose to myself and all those people with the 'Junior' tag: When do you stop being junior and become senior? Do you have to wait in line for the death of the senior for that promotion? Let's take George W. Bush 'Junior,' the forty-third president of America. Now, I understand why he was what he was. He was always a junior and never senior. But let's not forget Senior, Junior's father and the forty-first president of America. Whoops, that's an oxymoron. However, in defence of Junior, he was only following in his father's footsteps. Maybe that's the problem of naming your offspring after yourself: they have to continually prove that they are as good or better. Is this a genuine imitation? Sorry, another oxymoron!

Australians have a simpler way that removes much frustration when trying to remember a person's name. Basically, you can call nearly every person 'mate', which removes lots of embarrassing moments when you have forgotten a person's name. You can just say, 'How are you and the family, mate?' The only rule is, please don't forget your girlfriend or wife's name and try and get away with calling her or introducing her as 'mate'. That's nearly as bad as calling an Australian lady Sheila! However, to give you a little history lesson, I shall say the following. To live in Australia is to be with Australians, meaning people who live in Australia. You will soon learn the importance of 'mateship'. Mateship is a major part of Australian living. Australians will call a complete stranger 'mate' and say it in such a manner that the person will feel relaxed. Mates in Australia don't look for rewards or praise when they assist each other. A good mate is someone who never asks questions but is there through good times and bad. If you look at Australia's history over the last two hundred years, there are many tales about mates risking and giving their lives. It's not because they are heroes or braver than anyone else but just because the word 'mate' in Australia, in my opinion, means you are committed to assist.

Here's an example of this: In 1990, my mother died. I was working on a construction site at the time, so when my wife told me, I informed my employer and went home. Within hours, my employer had paid the airfare for me to go to the funeral, which was in England. The next day, one of the fellows from site visited my house. His exact words were, 'How are you, mate?' He gave me a card, which had been signed by all the blokes on site, including people who I had never met personally. Inside the envelope was $1,800 and in big words, 'She'll be right.' There was no need for me to say thank you or apologize when I left the room, eyes watering, as mates don't have to say anything.

Then there's the legendary tale of the Anzacs (Australian and New Zealand Army Corps), whose mate-ship created courage beyond their call. 'Anzac' was devised in 1915, reputedly by a New Zealand signaller, as a telegraph code name, and it was adopted by General Birdwood. In April of that year, he selected and named 'Anzac Cove' as the landing site on the Gallipoli Peninsula. The battle at Gallipoli subsequently became known as the Anzac campaign and resulted in the death of 8,141 Australians.

Legends are told of the bravery of young men and women who have served our nation beyond the call of duty, and their bravery is remembered each year on 25 April, which is our national Remembrance Day. 'Anzac' soon came to mean any Australian or New Zealand soldier, regardless of whether they had fought at Gallipoli or not. As well as implying fortitude and bravery, the word signified a physical type – tall, bronzed, and fit. In today's environment, you may hear a person say someone has the spirit of an Anzac, meaning a person who goes forward in times of trouble without considering their own safety with the aim of assisting or saving others.

The following is an excerpt from *Australian Geographic* (1999, vol. 1., p. 19), taken from an article about how and why Australian diggers get together on Anzac Day.

When Bob Dean, a barrel-chested bear of a man, beamed, said 'G'day,' and extended his hand, I almost winced in anticipation. Instead, his hand, hard and horny and big as a ham, enclosed mine with gentle warmth. He and his offsider, Mick Mensforth, the World War II digger who had raised and lowered the flag at the dawn service, invited me to join them for breakfast at Hay Service Club. I watched in awe as they ignored the din and devoured heaps of crispy bacon and fried eggs, beef sausages awash with Worcestershire sauce, toast and mugs of steaming tea. 'Siddown, son, siddown,' Bob said. 'Get stuck in. Never know,' he laughed, 'Might be y' last.'

Each year, Bob travels more than 100km north from his farm at Wakool to attend Hay's five minute Anzac dawn service with Mick. 'Wouldn't be Anzac Day without me an' Mick together.' In 1947, with the railway employees on strike, Bob cycled to Hay over clay roads just to be with his mate. 'Come through a lot, Mick an' me,' Bob said. 'The bloody heat, the bloody cold. That's what it's about … sharing'. The war made us mates, see? Mates is like … brothers, only closer.' How I envied that mateship, forged in the madness of war and nurtured over half a century, and their ability to look back and laugh like larrikins. 'The war taught us to make the most of our lives cause you never know when your time's up,' Bob said. 'Might be a bullet. Might be a shell or bomb. Might be a bloody bus crossing the road. The war taught us to value life, to live every day as if it might be our last.'

So please don't be offended if your name is pronounced incorrectly. There are worse things happening every second of the day. By all means, be proud of your name if you wish, or change it as you feel fit, if your parents lacked imagination or had too much. I would also say to parents, be kind when selecting your child's name, as they'll have to live with it until they are old enough to change it. And if an Australian calls you 'mate', don't be offended. Smile and think of what I have written above, as it means more than what most people think. But then again, it's just a name.

I shall finish this chapter with two quotations that could be linked to this chapter and are about names.

I always have trouble remembering three things: faces, names, and – I can't remember what the third thing is.

—Fred Allen

Call things by their right names – Glass of brandy and water! That is the current, but not the appropriate name; ask for a glass of liquid fire and distilled damnation.

—Robert Hall

Laugh and smile lots, as this is the medicine of life.

CHAPTER 10

In this chapter, I'll be sharing with you an entry from my diary. Ready to join me in a political discourse in John's world? Here we go!

The United States brags about its political system, but the President says one thing during the election, something else when he takes office, something else at midterm and something else when he leaves.

—Deng Xiaoping

Welcome to John's thoughts and rantings for the day. I don't write to antagonise politically-savvy people but offer an opinion on how I am ashamed of most governments around the world. On 17 July 2014, MH17 was shot down. To me, this was an act of terrorism, and I shall say that the person, group, or country responsible is cowardly. Such an act does not improve anything; it's madness. So I repeat, I am ashamed of those powerful governments and saddened by the fact that they lack the ability to truly govern. As I am ranting, I shall also say that the people of this world need to take time to truly analyse the policies and false promises given due to selfishness and the 'me, me, me' attitude. Yes, I am talking about myself and you, the reader. As we live in a country that allows us to vote, we should use that right.

Governments in the West, in my opinion, are elected on promises never kept and excuses that are continually made. Why aren't these promises kept? They always point fingers at previous governments. There is always a financial crisis that happens, may happen, or will happen, and the voters continue to complain. But to whom? We, the voters, may listen to all the hot air, but may we never accept it. Therefore we, the voters, could be a major part of the issue. Generally people do not want governments that make hard decisions, which have the potential to cost them money in increased taxes. Governments will continually argue that they must drastically reduce the budget deficits, decrease the nation's debt, and attack high unemployment. In principle the voters would agree, but the question that is not explained is the how and why.

Imagine a government that said, 'We can give you nothing, and in fact, we shall not be able to guarantee the status quo.' We, the people, would simply not accept this, as the elected government's job is to give, not to hold back. Maybe that's why they don't tell us the truth, as in the whole truth and nothing but the truth. That would mean no votes, and they need our votes.

This is where clever speech writers are employed to write lengthy speeches that are designed to say what the voters want to hear, without saying anything or really committing to anything. I don't want to sound unkind, but consider the following statement: The whole truth and nothing but the truth. This statement just doesn't sound right when politicians come to mind. You may think differently and call up the names of some great leaders and politicians, but were they really 100 per cent honest and truthful? I shall let you explore that thought.

Let's not generalise, as I am sure there are honest and truthful politicians somewhere out there in this great big world of ours. It's just hard to name them. My compassionate side is telling me to be kind, so in their defence, I might argue that most politicians go into politics with good intentions, thinking they can make a change. Maybe it is the political parties and the political system that restrict, and in some cases corrupt, their actions. Under this influence, the politicians may cease to strive for what they believed would be good for their electorate and country. It may even be those parties that are less than honest and truthful when dealing with the general public. Perhaps they make the politician their puppet and the voice of their party.

It is understandable that all governments want to stay in power. However, for this to happen, they need to stay popular, so that they have to promise to give. What they promise shall depend on the electorate or corporation that has voted and backed them to gain power. This is a never-ending process of gambling, auctioning, and selling, but never telling the truth, as the truth would be like a really bad dose of wicked medicine. No one likes bad medicine. We, the voters, would never accept them telling us we need a hard lesson, which may mean higher interest rates, more taxes, and less handouts.

Governments, in my opinion, have a tendency to procrastinate and postpone unpopular policies in order to be re-elected. As a result, the country's debt increases, unemployment climbs, and more and more people suffer. Or, should I say, some people suffer while some get richer. All this while governments do what governments do, which is argue, blame, and procrastinate. None of this fixes the problems at hand. What is guaranteed is that a problem that's left alone will not go away but be left for future generations to clean up.

Maybe, and I say maybe, it is because we, the voters, will not accept a government that actually makes those hard decisions and governs. Maybe we, the voters, forget that a government is mandated to govern.

Neither here, nor there, nor anywhere?

—Randall E Auxier

Whoops! Maybe I am wrong. Maybe we would allow a government to govern if we could find one that had the balls to be transparent and show the people of the country and world how much of a mess the country is really in. But no, this would cause chaos! People would demand change from a democracy to a dictatorship, or was it a

dictatorship to a democracy? Again, I may be just ranting, as one does after reading the world news that shows the unrest of millions of people demanding change.

Thinking aloud, what does democracy bring? Peace? Development? Freedom? Or just another confused and dysfunctional group of politicians and greedy individuals? I think what countries need to develop and we, the people of the world, need to understand, is that we need discipline more than democracy.

It's a fact that the countries and the people of the world are not equal. I would love to say they are, but I am not a politician, so why lie?

The exuberance of democracy leads to an undisciplined and disorderly condition. How depressing I sound, and the people of the free world will shout, 'You're wrong!' Wrong I may be, but I'm considering and thinking of the land of freedom and cookies, the country that now rides shotgun over the world in the name of keeping balance and keeping peace. I am talking about the land of freedom, the country that believes it is always right. This country is America, the land of milk and honey and, let's not forget, freedom! The freedom to kill – sorry, I meant to say the freedom to bear arms, which in my mind makes no sense. Tick, tick, tick. Here is another report of a teen or adult going wild, shooting innocent people. Each time that this happens, we ask ourselves, 'Why does this keep happening? What is the root cause?' I never see the true root cause in the paper. I only ever read about the underlying causes, such as that the person is crazy or a radical.

I have never read in the paper that such people commit crimes due to laws that give the freedom to buy and carry guns. It is part of their constitution. Even when their president, the most powerful leader in this world (In the minds of Americans, anyway), tries to introduce new gun laws, he fails. The voters across this crazy land shout, 'Never!' And politicians block new legislation. Why? Because they are selfish and gutless individuals who do not want to make decisions that would be unpopular and maybe reduce future votes, limiting their party from gaining office again.

I think the ultimate test of the value of a political system is whether it helps a society to establish conditions which improve the standard of living for the majority of its people while enabling the maximum amount of personal freedom for those that live within that country. I do not mean to confuse you, as it sounds like I am now promoting the West, which I am not. I am promoting any society or country, East, West, North, or South, that offers the most stable society for people and future generations to live in and die of natural causes in.

What I am saying is, we need to really consider the best governments across all countries, be it a democracy, republic, democratic republic, dictatorship, or even communism and stop promoting the idea that one system fits all.

What do I think of Western civilization? I think it would be a very good idea.

—**Mahatma Gandhi**

A good government and society is one that promotes fair play for all. I will continually promote that all people are equal and need to be treated as equals. However, equality depends on the country that you live in, whereby some people shall achieve more than others. This may be due to their physical or mental capacity or to the opportunities they receive. But it can also be due to policies that favour some over others. People's decisions can also be influenced by their family, friends, or group connections. But this is not new. It may be unfair or maybe not, depending on how they use their influence.

Moving away from looking at individuals and focusing more on countries, I would say that fair play, to me, is simple. No country should attack another or impose their beliefs or cultural norms on others. All people of the world should be given equal opportunities in education and medical benefits. Everyone should understand that to be the best, you must work hard and always do your best.

Therefore, we should never limit high achievers or try to suppress their brilliance. If this means they have to leave their country, let them leave. Then, other countries should accept them with open arms. I feel all countries need to reward high achievers and not hold back.

Innovation needs to flourish, and entrepreneurs need to be encouraged. Failure should not be ridiculed or punished, as in many cases, failure is necessary to succeed and grow.

John, you are ranting! Yes, I am, but we, the voters, need to rant a little more. Maybe then governments will better understand what we need. People need free education, medical care, and equal opportunities. People need a fair go for all, without any form of discrimination, including positive discrimination.

We need to understand that competition is good; it should be promoted and not destroyed by a large monopoly or unethical governments. Again, these are just my views. I do not think any government currently has all the answers, but I do like and could even promote Singapore, where capital punishment is in place and will be used. The country promotes democracy, but it is democracy with discipline. I also think they understand that to get the best out of politicians, you must pay for the best. That's why their leaders were recruited for their ability to lead and not selected by interested groups or due to connections with an association, union, or industry.

Corruptions start when we see, but do not recognize ... Or we recognise and do nothing!

—JRC. Mr John

Governments and voters must accept that we need to recruit leaders that are capable, competent, and willing to make some very hard and unpopular decisions. But for this to happen, they should be paid good salaries, equivalent to those of business leaders running successful multinational companies. We need leaders that work hard and run the government like a business, as government is the ultimate business; it is the business of the country and the people. If you pay people a fair wage, especially politicians and government employees including those in emergency services, the police, and the army, there will be no need for them to seek other means of payment, such as bribes or, worse, closing their eyes and brains and becoming a puppet. It is my opinion that elected officials should be held accountable and imprisoned if found to be corrupt.

Politicians need to understand that they are accountable for their actions or lack of action, the same way corporate law holds company directors accountable. Many directors across the world have faced legal charges and imprisonment. Australia and other countries have introduced the legal category of corporate manslaughter. Maybe, as I said above, if we held our politicians accountable for their actions and lack of action, they would act more responsibly and do a better job. This would include no longer wasting money to keep a few happy and the majority in shackles. I, as a voter, ask no more than that the people in government be honest, transparent, and willing to make decisions, even the hard ones. Lastly, they should stop treating the people of their countries as fools.

The elected government needs to be strong, and the people within governments have to be strong, caring, committed, honest, and disciplined. This sounds like an impossibility when I consider current politicians across the world.

However, we should not forget the real policy makers and those who really run governments. I am talking about the professional bureaucratic civil servants. They hold positions no matter what government is in power. These people need to be competent to ensure we have efficient administration. Oh, one last thing. As Lee Kuan Yew said, 'Business and countries need strong leaders, efficient administration, excellent communication and discipline.' I agree. Maybe this would stop the chaos.

I understand Deng Xiaoping said if 200,000 students have to be shot, shoot them, because the alternative is China in chaos for another 100 years ...

—Lee Kuan Yew

I am not sure if I could ever understand how any government could turn guns onto its own people. But read history and you will learn that most countries and governments have done this. It is about making the hard decisions. If I were going to look at China and consider the quotation above, from one of the greatest leaders (in my opinion), Lee Kuan Yew, I would say that maybe Deng understood the step process and knew he had to release the grip on his people and open China to Western ways. However, he also understood this had to be done in stages. Given the changes that have occurred in China in the past ten years, the government understands (in my opinion) that their governing style will need to be changed to ensure the chaos that Deng was so concerned about does not occur in the future.

I travel the world, and I can say that when in China, I do feel safe. In fact, I think it is safer than America and other Western countries that promote freedom of individuality while also allowing individuals to carry guns and promoting a permissive society where open and free sexuality is accepted as normal.

Humanitarians and human rights groups say it is wrong to harshly punish people and lobby for 'capital punishment' to be outlawed. I agree. We all deserve to be treated fairly. However, when innocent people are threatened and killed due to others being stronger, then that person, group, or government, in my opinion, if found guilty has no rights, as they lost all their rights when they elected to stop being human by raping, molesting, and killing innocents.

I would agree with Singapore, Malaysia, China, and other countries that use capital punishment on individuals that are found guilty for specific crimes. Taking anyone's life is wrong, but criminals, thugs, and government officials that prey on the weak need to know they will receive a punishment that fits their crime. If it means hard labour, caning, capital punishment, or being locked away forever to prevent another person being harmed, hurt, molested, raped, or killed, so be it. They do not need TV, and they do not need the comforts of home. This is not their home; it is prison.

What do you think? Is it fair for innocent people to fear going out?

Do we want our government to be strong and make the hard decisions, even when they are not popular?

We must combine the toughness of the serpent and the softness of the dove, a tough mind and a tender heart.

—Martin Luther King. Junior.

Another thought written a few days ago: The evil of war is not the physical wounds but the mental wounds, where a person becomes a head with his soul ripped out, a mind that cannot rest or stay still, as the darkness of his sorrow shall never heal.

2 November 2013: I awake thinking I have a nosebleed, as my pillow and sheets are covered in blood. I wipe at the stains with both hands, only to realise it was a dream. In my mind, it was real. As I settle and close my eyes, my thoughts are now of waters rushing over rocks. *What am I thinking?* I ask myself, and from the storage space of my memory emerges a picture. It is Alice, from *Alice's Adventures in Wonderland,* as she got swept away in an ocean of tears. Should I be disturbed or accept we are allowed to be mad within our own space, as mad as the Mad Hatter? This is my mind. A little madness, silliness, and daydreaming is the thing that allows me to keep my sanity.

Stories of the past, historical events, and daydreams of the future become an ocean made up of tears of humans past, present, and future. We cry so much. Is it for joy, sorrow, or disbelief at how we humans can be so special, creative, kind, and even loving? But as the wind changes, we can become evil.

I pray for all the people of this world. I hope that one day we can live in peace, where our only desire is to live a long and healthy life and where we can love every person. I pray for the people who lost their lives on MH 17 in July 2014 and their family and friends who will never understand why. I pray for all the people across the world who have suffered physical or mental pain, due to the actions of another. I pray that I can become a better person and all people can do the same. I pray that we will see goodness and kindness and that we will learn to forgive, forget, and move forward to a better world, where peace and harmony shall be given to all.

By three methods we may learn wisdom: First, by reflection, which is noblest; Second, by imitation, which is easiest; and third, by experience, which is the bitterest.

—Confucius

CHAPTER 11

12 Months and Still Writing

Quiet minds cannot be perplexed or frightened but go on in fortune or misfortune at their own private pace, like a clock during a thunderstorm.

—Robert Louis Stevenson

Tick, tick, tick. The hands of my watch and all the clocks around the world are moving. 'Happy New Year' were the last words I heard before my head hit the pillow. Thump, thump, thump. My head feels like it's in a vice. Should I scream? Should I cry? Or should I realise that alcohol is having its wicked way with my weaker brain cells? My theory is, human cells die or fail to remain strong and functioning because they are the weaker cells – just like when a wild animal wandering across the plains falls behind, making itself available as an easy target for vicious predators. Depending how weak or strong you are, one bottle of alcohol may lead to another and another, whereby the vicious predator is now allowed to attack your wallet and health. Or you could just be killing the weak cells and helping brewery workers to keep their jobs. See, there is always a positive side!

Or could it be this weaker than weak living thing is stronger than the rest? Are these cells giving their life to save the others? With this in mind, I say thank you to all the weak cells that have given their lives to save my stronger cells. Without their sacrifice, I would not have the ability to write this drivel today. Note to self: Send forty copies of my first book, *Bring Me a Higher Life*, to Thailand, where I will be delivering a keynote address to motivate a group of operational managers.

Now that my brain is coming back to life after being in a self-induced state of shock – or, should I say, hung-over from one too many New Year's good wishes – a second thought comes to mind. My second book was printed for Christmas, and the response I have received back is… none. Does this mean that after it was unwrapped, it now sits alone on a shelf, collecting dust? Or are the readers in utter shock that such words could get published? Well, the moment of truth finally came. I was tired of waiting for my publisher to put my words into a book, especially as the manuscript had been completed eighteen months ago and the agreement contract signed over twelve months ago. *Wait no more!* I thought, so I designed the cover, formatted the contents, and sent it to the printer, with the title *Table for Two, Sex Not Included.*

A special thank you must go to my dear friend Yarlian. That reminds me, the publishing house organised an author's tea on Saturday, 4 January, so I shall attend, hand over my completed copy, and ask them what they think.

However, I should not complain, as this is my second book to be published. News flash! It's my second book published and released on Amazon as an e-book. The title is the same, but the cover design was changed from being a simple black and gold, like the Bible, to a more serene image. It actually looks good, but you'll have to buy it and see for yourself.

However, with luck, the one I am writing now will be the one that captures more of my thoughts, abilities, and energy. I hope to stand strong, offer new insights into how I think, and also make you, the reader, think.

I like nonsense, it wakes up the brain cells. Fantasy is a necessary ingredient in living, it's a way of looking at life through the wrong end of a telescope. Which is what I do, and that enables you to laugh at life's realities.

—Dr Seuss

Random blurb: Another year has passed, and, believing that we should not waste a second, I am up at the break of dawn. I drink my coffee, swim twenty lengths in the pool, and go out for a walk to collect news of the New Year. This is the year of the horse in Chinese astrology, and the horse year is considered a fortunate one that brings luck and good things.

With this in mind, I galloped with reins in hand and hope within my heart to read news from around the world, believing that the wizard of peace and harmony would have cast a magical spell. Sigh. Maybe tomorrow, as all I saw today in the newspapers was bad and depressing, plus way too many advertisements tempting me to buy things that I do not want or need. Let's hope the year of the horse will bring good things to all. If there was a wizard, I'd ask him to cast a spell on the governments of the world and those ineffective politicians, so they will properly understand what a government is or what it ought to be.

In case a politician reads this, though, and before the wizard casts a spell, I shall say, 'Mr Politician, you have been elected and employed to serve the people of the country, meaning everyone, not a selected few. So please listen up and then serve!'

Fear not! I will write here. The newspapers are wrong, and we, the readers, have misread these articles of doom and gloom. All that is happening is part of human evolution. Change has to occur, in order for us to advance, and humans have always adapted to change. That's why we have survived. OK, we are slowly killing each other and destroying our environment, but we have always done that, so why change? I hear in louder than loud voices, echoing throughout my brain, don't change course now! Human genius will provide! A strange thing to say, perhaps, but it's just my opinion. We humans have continually believed that our superior brains and our ability to adapt shall ensure everything will be all right. But if that doesn't work, never fear, as I'm sure the believers will say, 'Trust in your faith!' Do I sound sarcastic? Let's think: yes.

Whoops! That's OK. I answered the question without giving you a text box to complete. I do not knock optimism, nor do I say any person should not believe and have faith in whatever they like. In fact, I promote both! All I am saying is, blind faith, closing our eyes, and saying nothing will not help this wonderful and beautiful planet much for future generations. Now I have even scared myself, as I'm not sure if we can trust human genius and the Almighty to fix what we humans have knowingly destroyed and are destroying. Tick, tick, tick. Time for another coffee and a few minutes of meditation before I tackle Kuala Lumpur traffic to meet the publisher.

Sigh, I never made it to the meeting. I drove for over two hours, only to get totally lost. Should I blame the GPS? It sure gave me a great journey but not the way to the publisher's. On the bright side, however, I did get to see areas of Kuala Lumpur that I had not been to before. But to remove my frustrations of not meeting the publisher, a movie is required.

I love escaping through movies and finding those inner-self moments. What I mean here is having the ability to turn off. It may sound strange, but I generally allow myself to move into the movie. This allows my imagination to run free and explore more than what I see on the screen. Escapism, in any legal form, is good. I usually treat myself to tickets to the Gold Cinemas, which have large and comfy reclining chairs. So if the movie is bad, I can fall asleep in comfort.

Today, we watched *The Delivery Man,* which is the story of a friendly underachiever, David Wozniak. His mundane life is turned upside down when he finds out that he fathered 533 children through sperm donations he made twenty years earlier. To add to his troubles, he owes the mob (mafia) thousands of dollars and has been rejected by his pregnant girlfriend. You may ask why his beautiful and successful girlfriend would want to him, but after explaining the premise, that would be a little bit of a silly question. However, back to the movie. Just as he thought things could not get any worse, he receives a lawsuit from 142 of the 533 young adults who want to know the identity of their biological father. It was an interesting movie. If you listen to the words and enjoy being lost within a silly tale, it can make you feel good when you leave. Or, I should say, it made *me* feel good, as I like happy endings. Whoops! I think I've just given the ending away!

Happiness is not something ready made. It comes from your own actions.

—Dalai Lama

Tick, tick, tick. Unexplainable or illogical thoughts – where do they come from, especially past midnight? Is this the time when memories come alive? Or do they go to sleep, allowing neurons to interact and look for answers to the questions that were not answered by their owner? Maybe they were answered, and the billion or more neurons are busy working the night shift to store those memories away but having fun while they work. They send images through dreams that scare you, excite you, or make you feel as if you are falling, but then you wake up, never hitting the ground.

Does the brain ever sleep? Do those beautiful little neurons rest and gain strength to manage our brain cells that use biochemical reactions to receive, process, and transmit information? In simple terms, a neuron is a cell specialised to conduct and generate electrical impulses and to carry information from one part of the brain to another. As I am writing this, I am listening to 'Tubular Bell' by Mike Oldfield. Is that why I can remember such drivel?

If my memory serves me correctly, our brains never sleep, and I remember reading somewhere that we humans can have up to four to five dreams a night! The only one we remember is the one being 'played' when we wake up. If this is correct, and accepting that on average we sleep eight hours a night and we live to eighty years old, we will sleep for about 26.6 years of this life.

That's a lot of sleep, and if we do dream four to five times per night, that would mean we have over 130,000 dreams in our lifetime. Oh, shit! That means at my age, I would have had over 90,000 dreams! Bugger! Now I will not sleep tonight trying to remember the best dream I ever had! Interesting thought. Well, I think it is interesting. I can now call every person a dreamer. And even better, I am not alone. So don't worry if you dream. Enjoy them. And remember, a dream is just a dream until we wake up and make it a reality.

Dreaming or daydreaming is free and sometimes amusing and fun. So next time you dream of a rainbow and that pot of gold at the end, keep your optimist hat on. You could say it was just a dream, or you could say it is a vision of things to come. However, if you are having a reoccurring dream and that dream is disturbing you, maybe you should seek professional advice. But again, this is your choice. Dreams are just that: dreams. Again, that is my opinion, and I am sure many shall say I am wrong. Right or wrong, I enjoy dreaming, especially daydreaming. These are the dreams that I have some control over, and where I create imaginary scenes or scenarios. My daydreams never turn into nightmares, as no one likes a nightmare. What I shall say here is, a dream only remains a dream until we do something to turn it into a reality. This is getting too deep. Let's think of rainbows and become light-hearted instead.

What does a rainbow represent? Not in its truest form, but as we see it. Could it be the freedom to explore, express ourselves, or just be alone and allow our creativity to rest? Does a rainbow sing to your eyes, just as music is a sight for your ears? The colours of a rainbow always appear in the same order: red, orange, yellow, green, blue, indigo, and violet. How wonderful it is that nature offers us all its riches for nothing. As the sun pours light across our planet, in perfect harmony a heavenly dance is performed. I shall call this dance 'the rainbow dance', as the sun sends its light to partner with water droplets in the atmosphere. Then there's the invisible choreographer demanding a perfect circle, which we are only allowed to see a part of. But that part is beautiful, as it arches to reach out where more and more can see.

Try to be a rainbow in someone's cloud.

—Maya Angelou

Enjoy the rainbow dance and the beauty as it is. Don't expect more or less, and stop wasting your time looking for the end of the rainbow and for that pot of gold. As said, it is a perfect circle. So where is the beginning, and where is the end? Only you, the creator of the circle, knows. If this is your dream, maybe it is time for you to wake up and realise that the pot of gold at the end of the rainbow may never be found. If you keep going around in circles, like a dog chasing its tail, you will only catch it and then let it go so the game can start again. Everything in life is in some way connected, and generally, we are all looking for the same things: happiness, love, and a sense of belonging. What is sad is that during all the time we are chasing that rainbow, we may miss what we already have. Being content with who you are or what you have is not a bad thing; it is a magical thing.

You should stop chasing your tail or looking for help from others. Help yourself by being the person you want to be. If that means you want a pot of gold, then start working hard, as it will take hard work and commitment to gain success. Success in whatever we do does not come easy. If you want to be happy, then lighten up and be happy. Even the poorest of the poor can be happy, because success does not automatically make you happy. Even the richest people in the world are continually looking for something.

I shall end here by saying, stop looking for help from others. Help yourself by first identifying what you want and then taking the necessary steps to get it. All the self-help books in every bookshop in the world will not be able to tell you what you want in life. Only you truly know that. So stop wasting your money on books or seminars, looking for answers that you already know in your heart but maybe are too scared to admit. If you are reading a book or going to seminars to get ideas, gather inspiration, or even get motivated, that is fine, but don't lose sight of what the goal is. The goal, I believe, is to understand what it is you want and not what others are saying you want.

Change does not roll in on the wheels of inevitability, but comes through continuous struggle. And so we must straighten our backs and work for our freedom. A man can't ride you unless your back is bent.

—Martin Luther King, Jr.

Tick, tick, tick. Time is flying. I will say here that I have not been chasing my tail or going around in endless circles for the past thirty days, since I first started to write this chapter. I have been doing my day job and having time out with family and friends. So, my second job, which is to write, was put on hold until I felt the need to put pen to paper and explore my mind. Ah, here I am now, sitting in a hotel room in Vietnam. We came to celebrate the Tet lunar New Year with our Vietnamese family. The celebration can be traced back to myths and legends of the pre-Chinese period, which prevailed in an authentically Viet culture of the Bronze Age (first millennium BC) called the Red River Culture. Archaeological findings would suggest that this culture's population grew along the Red River Delta, the main river of North Vietnam. However, this chapter is not a history lesson on Vietnam but a mind dump, as all my chapters are. Hopefully, after reading my first two books, you would by now understand this. But again, I digress.

Do not take life too seriously. You will never get out of it alive.

—Elbert Hubbard

I would like to share a beautiful story, though I'm sure my writing won't give it justice. The story or myth that I shall try to capture is about a love affair between a dragon and fairy or a heavenly angel.

It is said that a water dragon had fallen in love with a fairy, and their love was so strong that they married. Never had such a thing been heard of or done before, but the marriage produced a hundred eggs. When hatched, the eggs produced a hundred sons, which was celebrated by both father and mother. However, as time went by, they realised that the differences between them, which made them attracted to each other, were now causing problems, particularly in terms of what their sons should learn. As the father was a creature of the water, he felt his sons should understand the richness of the seas, and he wanted them to live close to the coast. The mother, on the other hand, was from the land, and she wanted her children to understand the beauty of the highlands. So as to not destroy their love for each other or to upset their sons, they agreed to separate, taking fifty children each. They were never to marry again, as their hearts and souls were one and forever joined. The children that left with their mother, the fairy of the land, worked with nature and developed great skills to ensure they could protect their land. More importantly, they learnt from the land, so they could produce food for the future people to come. The sons of the father became coastal people. As the father did not want them to travel too far away from the water, he gave his sons the lessons of the sea. They worked with the sea to protect the land and harvested food from the sea to look after the future generations of people.

The love of the two parents never died, and they secretly met high in the skies to discuss the success of their sons. This success was even more apparent as one of the sons who went with the dragon father became the founder of the Hung Dynasty, the first king of Vietnam, which is thought to have existed from as early as 2769 BC until 100 AD. The fifty sons who went to the coast are considered to be the people of the Lac Kingdom. According to historians and archaeologists, the Lac were a coastal people who had developed a sophisticated wet rice agricultural society as early as 1500 BC. The Hungs, as depicted in mythology, were mountain people, who are believed to have had a reciprocal agreement with the Lac Kingdom, so that the Hungs protected the Lacs from aggressive mountain groups in return for rice and other crops grown on the coastal plains of the Red River. This created a joining of the land and sea and symbolised the love between a heavenly fairy and a noble water dragon.

This story takes on many forms, depending on the region in which it is being told. But what remains the same is the birth of the hundred children and how from these children came the birth of a great country, where the people of the ocean and land worked together and family bonds grew.

The love of family and the admiration of friends is much more important than wealth and privilege.

—Charles Kuralt

What do I see when I come to Vietnam for the Tet holidays? It is a time for families to come together, to enjoy the beginning of the next year, and also to show respect for family members who have gone from this world. Flowers and trees are purchased and put on display, Buddhist temples are visited, and many present goods as offerings and pray for the next year to be a good one.

It is custom that on the first day of the New Year, that being 31 January this year, 2014, people to eat vegetarian meals, as the eating of meat would mean killing an animal. So, vegetarian food is cooked early and first offered to relatives who have left this world. After chants and prayers are said, the food can be eaten. It is important that your ancestors do not go hungry on the other side. Therefore, you must ensure you correctly chant the person's name, date of birth, date of death, and relationship to you. This is not seen as an act to mourn the dead but a celebration of their lives. I shall add here that many Vietnamese people offer their food through prayer at every meal to relatives or ones they love who have left this world to wait in a better place. They wait for family to be re-joined, so prayers at mealtime are the Vietnamese way of sending love and ensuring loved ones are never forgotten and live on in their hearts.

At this time of the year, the house is cleaned, new clothes are bought, and people go to clean the burial grounds, so the entire family (even the deceased) can enjoy the beginning of a new year. If only it were a day when alcohol were also prohibited! But it is not, so I find myself sitting on a smaller-than-small chair outside Ngo's (my soul mate and wife) sister's house, showing respect by drinking all that is put in front of me. The copious amount of booze is destroying my weaker brain cells and not making the stronger ones feel very good. I should mention here that her sister and brother do not drink, so now I am expected to drink for the entire family to ensure that our relatives who have passed on do not go thirsty! It is a job I take very seriously.

Today is 1 February 2014, the day after Tet, and I must admit I needed vitamins and gallons of water throughout the night. I drank the Bababa (or, as written on the label, 333) beer like water over a seven-hour period yesterday. In fact, Nhu's sister calls beer 'John water'. The chemically enhanced substance tried to influence my over-indulging stomach to react, or maybe just drink some more. However, I shall say I put up a wonderful show, not spilling a drop as both hand and mouth worked in perfect sequence to ensure all the beer was consumed without a commercial break or rest. As the family kept bringing cold beers to ensure I and the deceased relatives were kept busy, to be honest, I feel a little tender. I know next year I shall sit on the same chair laughing and laughing some more, totally relaxed and feeling at home with my Vietnamese family as we eat and celebrate together. I shall take this moment to apologise to my brain and ask it to work hard to restore the memory loss that may have occurred as well as get ready to take the challenge on again in another twelve months.

In the long run, we shape our lives, and we shape ourselves. The process never ends until we die. And the choices we make are ultimately our own responsibility.

—Eleanor Roosevelt

---

31 January 2014 was another great day and a meaningful event for me, as my daughter turned thirty that day. She will celebrate this new age in the year of the horse, a fortunate year. As I have always said, I am a lucky man. I have lived a life that has allowed me to explore where I got lost but always find my way again. I may not have always taken the most direct route, and I've had to make a few U-turns along

the way, but I never gave up on my ultimate desire: to understand who I really am.

I am a normal-looking man who could be lost in a crowd, as I am of average size and appearance. This allows me to move without others even noticing me. I am not invisible in appearance but invisible in manners until I want to be seen, heard, or noticed. People who think they know me would say I am an extroverted person who needs to be the centre of attention. That is their perception. Those people who really know me, however, would say that I am a caring person who often puts others first but is a little crazy and eccentric too. This, again, is their perception. However, their perception is normally made up by what I portray or show, which I think can create confusion unless the person has known me for a long time. To explain this, I would say I respond quickly to my instincts when it comes to others. I use all my senses when making decisions, but I use both my heart and brain depending on the situation. It may be right or wrong, but that is me, and I am the only person who can explain myself. As I said before, I am an introvert who portrays the outward appearance of an extrovert. I can switch between these two personalities easily, as a chameleon does to protect itself without losing sight of who it really is. I am a feeling person who also has the ability to think, but I never do both at the same time, as it is my belief they should be separated. I use my senses, as I have learnt that if you are in sync with your senses, your intuition works better.

The teacher who is indeed wise does not bid you to enter the house of his wisdom but rather leads you to the threshold of your mind.

—Khalil Gibran

To close this chapter, I shall say that overindulgence and being curious are not good. After three wonderful days, my ever-ready battery that was turbo charged and had never gone flat had finally bottomed out. I feel like someone has just removed all the energy cells from my body. Worse still, instead of being allowed to rest and recharge, I am now having to be a Olympic sprinter to ensure this grown man does not have an accident! To make it worse, I came down with food poisoning. Why do I mention this? Well, I feel chapter 12 should be a chapter where I do research and look at food across the world, exploring the wonders and unusual titbits we consider our national delights.

CHAPTER 12

Food, Glorious Food

I'm very type-A, and many things in my life are about control and domination, but eating should be a submissive experience, where you let down your guard and enjoy the ride.

—Anthony Bourdain

'Please, sir, I want some more,' goes the famous line from *Oliver Twist*. The word 'more' in that sentence is echoed throughout the dining room. How dare that skinny, half-starved child ask for more? Doesn't he know that he has no rights apart from accepting and being thankful for whatever handout he is given? This was the mind set of times gone by, as it was believed that everyone, especially children, needed to understand their position and never question an adult and their rules. It was also believed that keeping people busy, including children, stopped their minds from wandering to places and positions above their means.

And why should Oliver complain? The children like him were the unwanted, the forgotten. The workhouses gave them a floor to sleep on and a meal, even if the food was only gruel that needed no teeth to chew but a stomach to take. A workhouse was a place that orphans or the poor were sent to in the past. How things stick in your mind. I can remember those specific words, written and later acted and sung in the musical *Oliver* in 1968. It was a British movie that won six Oscars at the forty-sixth Academy Awards, as well as many other awards, and I was only ten when I saw the movie for the first time.

Since that time, I have watched hundreds, maybe thousands of movies, but I clearly remember this one. As I write this, I am humming along with the music in my head, especially the song 'Food, Glorious Food'. I am making up the words as I go, including those tasty little things that I miss and want. These foods were not in or even considered in the original, as this is John's version of the song. Foie gras and cheese, red wine and port! 'What next?' is the question. 'An empty wallet or two,' I say, with a smile on my face.

The original words to the song were: 'Food, glorious food! Hot sausage and mustard! While we're in the mood -- Cold jelly and custard! Pea's pudding and saveloys! What next is the question? Rich gentlemen have it, boys --indigestion!'

As I try and sing this song, my mind drifts back to buying peas pudding and faggot at Addington Street in Ramsgate in the Pie and Earl Shop or walking to the high street to have a hot saveloy and minced meat pie … How my tastes have grown since those days. I would not consider myself rich in financial terms, but I have suffered indigestion, which I must say was due to overindulging.

Food, glorious food! Well, I'm not Oliver, nor am I a person who will astound you with knowledge of herbs and how wonderful they will make a dish taste. I am a punter, who over the years has had a long-lasting love affair with dining out and tasting different foods from around the world. I will say here, though, that I eat to live and do not live to eat. I enjoy all food.

I don't like food that's too carefully arranged; it makes me think that the chef is spending too much time arranging and not enough time cooking. If I wanted a picture, I would buy a painting.

—Andy Rooney

Before I discuss why I like to eat out or the type of food I enjoy, let's consider some of the foods that are considered delicacies from around the world. I live in Malaysia, and a favourite food throughout this region is durian, which is lovingly known as the king of fruits. I would say it is the smelliest of fruits, but it's nice if you block your nose before eating.

Then there's bird's nest soup, a soup that has literally been cooked from congealed bird spit. However, the menu at a Chinese restaurant will talk of the wonders that this stuff can do for your health. Yet it says nothing about a small bird coughing up a ball of phlegm, and really, this is what you are eating. We humans steal the nest of this charming little bird and sell it on for large amounts of money for others humans to eat gladly, without considering that it is a waste product of a little bird. Food, glorious food?

Or we could consider *balut*, a Filipino delicacy, which is a fertilised duck egg boiled alive and eaten in the shell. I am told it tastes nice, and the closest I got to eating one was cracking the shell. However, as I looked at it and saw a half-formed little bird looking back at me, I had to give it to my daring partner to eat. Sharing is caring, and she enjoyed it!

As balut was a little too adventurous for me (which is saying a lot, since I normally try most things because I believe I should not write about something unless I have tried it), I went for the century egg. It's a duck or quail egg that has been preserved in a saline solution for months. It's not bad. It has a weird creamy-jelly texture and tastes just like a regular egg. It looks like it has gone bad and is ready for retirement or the trash, so I was surprised that the taste was OK, especially with a little ginger.

I would recommend to any traveller passing through Hong Kong to visit markets that sell all types of insects, dried or fried. I am told that if I eat them, they shall improve my virility. In Vietnam I drank snake wine for the same reason, and in Indonesia I had a cup of overpriced coffee called kopi luwak, which is made by the coffee berries being eaten and then excreted by the Asian palm civet. Isn't it amazing how we humans love eating the waste products of animals? I believe this coffee is drunk across the world, I hope only drunk as a novelty. I thought it tasted like shit, or should I say terrible. But then, I am not a coffee connoisseur, merely a person who enjoys coffee.

I never drink coffee at lunch. I find it keeps me awake for the afternoon.

—Ronald Reagan

Some quotations make me smile. After reading the one above, I wondered if Reagan said this while he was an actor or as the president of America. I am sure he would have been a milk and cookies man and enjoyed dining, maybe not experimenting but just enjoying taking time out not being a cowboy or president of America.

However, that's enough of that. Let's get back to the food we eat and may never eat. I could have listed hundreds of things that I have tried and, if I am honest, some I have struggled with. Usually, when I come across unusual food, my eyes send warning signals to my brain. I overcome this by not looking, and I have even been known to close my eyes while I put something in my mouth. This allows my taste buds to do their job without any preconceived judgement. Another secret from John's guide to tasting new foods is, be ready to swallow quickly with a funny face. Forget the mandatory twenty chews. Swallowing it, to me, is more polite than spitting it out with an even funnier face.

The best thing about eating and being open to new things is the pleasure of trying. Sometimes, you will be surprised how nice those strange to look at things really are.

I travel lots with my work and also because I like visiting new places, so I am always intrigued with the national dishes of the countries I visit. They range from being ten out of ten to, sorry to say, boring and bland. However, in saying that, I am reminded that many are practical and some are extravagant. America promotes the hamburger as their national dish – obesity here we come! England goes for roast beef and Yorkshire pudding: traditional and safe, but not very adventurous.

Hungary has goulash, which is like a beef stew that is rich in flavour due to being cooked slowly. The spices used give it such a rich taste, which is even better if eaten on a cold night.

When I visited Korea, I really enjoyed bulgogi. It is a dish made up of thinly sliced prime cuts of meat that have been marinated in a mixture of soy sauce, sesame oil, garlic, onions, ginger, sugar, and wine and then grilled. Great! Now my mouth is watering.

When in Vietnam, you can't go without a bowl of pho, a Vietnamese noodle soup. I like the chicken, but beef is great too, especially for supper, after drinking and before going to bed. And I am lucky, as my wife makes the best pho.

I want my food dead. Not sick, not dying, dead.

—**Oscar Wilde**

In China I could name several dishes that I enjoyed, and many of those could be considered national dishes, like the Peking duck, wontons, chow mein noodles, and a few others. But one of my favourites is ma po tofu. This is a tofu that is served in a brownish-red sauce with ground beef, chopped green onion, and other spices. I am not sure what the spices are, but they taste very good. It fills you up without making you feel like your stomach is now a beach ball waiting to be popped.

In France, I am sorry to say, I normally over-indulge on cheese and breads. My favourites dishes in France are escargot cooked with garlic and parsley butter and bouillabaisse, which is a fish soup. You may be thinking, 'Fish soup? What's so special about that?' Well, what makes it different from other fish soups is the selection of Provençal herbs and spices in the broth, as well as how the fishes are added one at a time, in a certain order, and brought to a boil. The method in which the dish is served is also special. In Marseille, the broth is served first in a bowl, where you dunk bread. The seafood and vegetables are served separately on another platter. Oh, that was a great night! Special friends, good wine, and many laughs! And to be honest, I did not remember the name of the dish and had to ask a friend, as I always called it special French fish soup.

I, personally, think there is a really danger of taking food too seriously. Food should be part of the bigger picture.

—Anthony Bourdain

I could write much more about the dishes I have eaten and enjoyed while traveling, such as a simple cheese sandwich in London, after arriving back from Nigeria, or a frog that was slow-cooked in bamboo over an open fire in Vietnam. The list could go on and on.

But I find the experience of enjoying food is even more delightful when I'm in good company. This is particularly true when you're in the corner booth of a restaurant, where you feel comfortable and relaxed.

I think you have to be in the right mood for eating. Just because the food is great, does not always make for a great night. It takes more for you to truly enjoy the evening. It's the ambience. The feeling that surrounds you heightens the experience. This is because you have the full package that makes you want to come back for more and more.

Whoops! Sorry, Mr. Bumble and Widow Corney (the people who run the workhouse in *Oliver* and serve gruel, a non-tasty, unbalanced diet of boiled water with crushed grain). Poor Oliver Twist. Did he really want gruel, or was he just hungry for *more?* Sometimes more is needed, but sometimes more is gluttonous, and sometimes more is just more. So enjoy, and try to practice moderation in all things, apart from smiles and laughs.

I honestly believe we live in lucky times when it comes to food, as people are continuously moving and settling in new countries. The reason they move could fill another book. Whatever their reasons, they bring with them recipes for dishes that were passed down from generation to generation.

We are exposed to incredible dishes from around the world, and in most cases we can enjoy these dishes without leaving our own country. For example, Australia has over two hundred nationalities. The next time you visit Melbourne and stroll the streets, you will see food from across the world, and recipes will range from extraordinary to practical and tasty. I enjoy eating out as much as I enjoy eating at home, but eating out must be special, or why waste your money?

Ping-pong was invented on the dining tables of England in the 19th century, and it was called Wiff-waff! And there, I think, you have the difference between us and the rest of the world. Other nations, the French, looked at a dining table and saw an opportunity to have dinner; we looked at it and saw an opportunity to play Wiff-waff.

—Boris Johnson

I love the quotation above. When I think of England versus France, I would say the English would be happy having fish and chips in newspaper so they can eat quickly and get back to the TV remote, whereas the French are never in a rush when it comes to eating, as it is an event that should be enjoyed. However, in defence of the world's population and especially those fish and chip-eating Englishmen, it appears to me we are evolving and becoming more adventurous. We allow our taste buds to be exposed to new delights because people can now enjoy fabulous dining. This would not be considered fine dining but bloody good dining. We have so many choices and so many places to try. Competition is high, making the restaurateurs compete for business, trying their best to provide the best service, prices, and experience, so it's a win-win situation for food lovers.

But where to go? There are so many choices, which is great. But when there are lots of choices, it can also be a little confusing. I am a simple man, not in mind but in needs. So if a person were to ask me what is it that makes eating out so special, I would say it's the ingredients of life.

For starters, we all have different tastes, so the atmosphere must suit the mood and the food. The ambience in the restaurant and the service of the staff are some of the most important parts of dining. Please do not get me wrong: the food is important and needs to be tasty. After all, that is the reason you are dining out, to enjoy the food that is not available at home or to give yourself or your partners a break from the kitchen.

The choice is yours, so whether you choose a white-table clothed fine dining restaurant or a fast food outlet, it must be enjoyed. Is that an oxymoron? How could I put fine dining and fast food in the same sentence?

However, before I slap myself around, I must remember that we are all looking for different things when dining. As I look around a restaurant, I think lots about others and wonder what are they thinking or why they chose this restaurant or that place.

Only the diner knows why they picked that restaurant or place. If it is two young lovers, it's about feeling special and being able to relax and listen to each other or just enjoy a special moment in time. It is about not being disturbed constantly by a waiter who's asking if everything is OK. It is important to have enough time between dishes to ask those important questions or just stare into each other's eyes. This type of dining is about giving, so you can receive. What you receive may be different depending on the night, and I am not talking about the food, wine, or service from the restaurant. Use your imagination, please.

Then we have a totally different kind of dining: the family get-together. I am not talking about the good old BBQ, which will never be totally replaced. More and more, families are going to restaurants.

I, personally, find this an incredible opportunity to catch up with my children, as we all live busy lives in different countries. So it is nice when we are all together to make those moments special. We can all relax and just enjoy being together without worrying about who has to do what. We all have a singular task, not to enjoy the food but to go out, eat, and more importantly talk to each other without worrying about the TV removing our ability to communicate.

Look, I don't want to wax philosophic, but I will say that if you're alive you've got to flap your arms and legs, you've got to jump around a lot, for life is the very opposite of death, and therefore you must at very least think noisy and colourfully, or you're not alive.

—Mel Brooks

Good restaurant owners understand that their clientele have different needs. For example, when families dine, it's about making the table an extension of their home, where they can feel comfortable and chat, which often creates laughter.

Then, we must consider the business lunch. And yes, I often hear that these are outdated. All I can say is, I still see many businesses partaking in the finer things in life. But what are we looking for when there is business to be done over food? I, personally, always select a restaurant that suits the client. If you're not sure, ask. I always consider the noise level. There is nothing worse than trying to discuss a proposal and becoming frustrated due to the noise factor or other distractions.

I would select a restaurant that I have used before or that the client suggests. I would never take a chance on selecting a new restaurant, just in case the food or the wine selection is poor or, even worse, the staff are less than competent. When it comes to selecting a restaurant for business, I would say the competency of the restaurant's staff is my first priority.

I never go to the 'in place' or the 'must be seen in' place when selecting a restaurant to discuss business. It has been my experience that the crowd will be noisy and the restaurant will be busy. The 'must be seen' crowd will accept the noisy environment, and possibly you will need to wait longer to be served. Remember, you're not trying to buy the restaurant or impress the client with the amount of personalities that can be seen.

In closing, I would say that what I always look for is a place that can be enjoyed by all and make every person feel special and comfortable. The ambience must be right to ensure it is a memorable occasion. No matter if it is business or pleasure, the enjoyment of eating must suit the mood and the occasion.

I believe in pink. I believe that laughing is the best calorie burner. I believe in kissing, kissing a lot. I believe in being strong when everything seems to be going wrong. I believe that happy girls are the prettiest girls. I believe that tomorrow is another day and I believe in miracles.

—Audrey Hepburn

I believe in myself and the person next to me. I believe all food should be tried, even that half-formed baby duck egg… or maybe not. The next chapter, or should I say next several chapters, shall explore what I consider to be the most important thing: believing in yourself and not relying on others to tell you that you are OK. We do not need the accolades of others to live a good life, as long as we live our life.

I hope you'll enjoy it. But before I go, please read Audrey Hepburn's quotation one more time, as it is nice to read and even nicer to believe.

CHAPTER 13

Nobody

To be nobody but yourself in a world which is doing its best, night and day, to make you everybody else means to fight the hardest battle which any human being can fight; and never stop fighting.

—E. E. Cummings

How did I go from talking about food to writing this chapter, which I've titled 'Nobody'? Well, it's because I can. Moreover, you may be feeling hungry right now, and I can't offer you food within these pages of text. However, I can feed your mind. So let's explore how some people do not consider themselves valuable. I watched a TV show the other day called *The Wahlbergs,* and I was impressed when brothers Mark and Donnie, who are both popular actors, praised their brother Paul (who's a chef) and credited him as being the real talent in the family. And let's be honest, without his famous brothers, would anyone even think of Paul as someone worth taking note of?

Of course he is, and that's the point! We are all someone to somebody, even when we don't think we are. Have you ever heard someone say, 'I'm nobody', or have you yourself started a sentence with 'I'm just' or, 'I'm only'? Firstly, I'd like to shout out and say, Everyone is someone! There's no such thing as a nobody! From that very first breath, we are destined to be someone. It doesn't matter who you are or which socioeconomic group you come from. You are someone, and you are special.

Then, as you grow, you evolve due to the opportunities you've received. How quickly you evolve or advance shall depend on you as an individual and your desires. I am sure that some people, including myself in my earlier years, think that they are less worthy than others. Some people don't consider their work or occupation to be as important as others. So instead of saying with pride, 'I am a...' they end up saying, 'I'm just a...' If that person were talking to me, I would normally stop them and highlight that we cannot all be brain surgeons or inventors. If we were all Einstein or Steve Jobs or Bill Gates, then who would clean our roads, build our homes, look after the old, teach the young, or drive the buses, trains, or taxis? Remember, there are many links in a chain, and each link is just as important as the others.

Oh, bugger! I just remembered this great story I once heard. President Kennedy made an unannounced visit to NASA. When he came across a man in overalls, he asked the man, 'And what do you do here?' The man, who was a janitor, replied, 'I am here to help you put a man on the moon.' And he was right. He was part of the team needed to put a man on the moon. He could have answered, 'I am just a janitor,' but he didn't. He saw his job as more than that. Every person is somebody, and it is up to us all to realise this. You don't have to wait for someone else to say, 'You're OK.' In fact, don't expect someone to say this; it may never happen. People are too busy chasing their own tails, going around in circles, and losing themselves in their own self-destructive and materialistic space. Sadly, many people are merely trying to navigate their own journey, with minimum consideration for others. They do not see or care about the negative energy they are distributing.

I am sure some of you may now be thinking, 'But why don't we care for others more? Or slow down and take the time to appreciate what others are doing?' Whoops! You're forgetting that we're all individuals and quite selfish.

Therefore, with this in mind, let's connect and create a world filled with connections. This is so easy. Start by smiling at a stranger and saying hello, or helping another person when they need help, or offering your seat to an elderly person. Being kind and giving without expecting anything in return is connecting. These simple little things cost us nothing but I am sure will make us feel better about ourselves. Remember, we are not looking or wishing for accolades from another; we must simply agree to respect ourselves for what we have and for what we have done. After all, every little thing we do, and do not do, can make a difference to us and others.

In oneself lies the whole world and if you know how to look and learn, the door is there and the key is in your hand. Nobody on earth can give you either the key or the door to open, except yourself.

—J. Krishnamurti

Shuffling a deck of cards with the expectation that you can predict all fifty-two cards as they turn is like expecting that every day we live will be perfect. We never truly know how our day, and much less our lives, will turn out. If we concentrate and identify a path early enough, then planning and preparation may reduce some of the disappointments that may come our way. However, even this may not be enough to stop us from thinking, 'What if?' much later in life.

However, as my glass is always half full, I have no regrets over what has happened in my life. I came to understand many years ago that life is a journey, along which I am sure that we all shall make mistakes and even hurt people. What I hope is that the majority of us will do our best, never deliberately or intentionally hurting anyone. As I write the above, I can reflect on fifty-seven years of life. And in general terms, I've just accepted what came my way and not pushed back by thinking of the consequences or what-ifs.

I was living the life, which I thought was my life, and enjoying all the opportunities as they arrived without hesitation or guilt. James Brown, the great singer and songwriter, once sung, 'It's a Man's World.' I've personally never felt that it's a man's world. Instead I've felt that it's a woman's world, one that I have been allowed to participate in and enjoy while living in a world that I've created for myself: John's world.

An explanation to the above statement is not required for those who have lived their lives. Whether man or woman, they will understand that moments come and go. Some will be enjoyed by men, and others will be enjoyed by women. And some will be enjoyed by both. It shouldn't be a competition. Nor should gender, intelligence, or gender diversity be a competition or one-sided. Let's face life's challenges as individuals and do our best, without trying to be something we are not, whatever that is.

Accepting life and the opportunities that come with it will fulfil our needs – or should I say, it has fulfilled *my* needs. Our internal desire to remain energised requires us to remain plugged in to whatever energy source gives us the most energy. Life cannot be lived to its full potential if we are not energised. Energy gives us the power to take on the next challenge, whatever that may be. So plug in and stay charged for the moments that will fill your scrapbook of life. Allow yourself to rock and smile about it when you're old.

Whoops! I just had a thought. Maybe there is a nobody in every person's life. Let's think. Could it be the person that we see and describe to our partners or friends as 'Oh, that's nobody,' when we get a phone call from them? Ah, have I just worked out who nobody is? It's someone who we know, but we don't want others to know that we know them. Sorry if I'm confusing you, but it's simple. The nobody we're talking about here is somebody that we want to talk to but do not want others (and especially those special few) to know about. So we say, without guilt, that it is nobody.

However, that nobody is someone. He or she must be important, as we protect them and ourselves by saying they are nobody, making us nobody.

This is not protection. This is denial, as there should never be a person in our lives that we cannot mention or name. Those people you have said are no-one are someone, and maybe more than you may wish to admit.

Cognitive psychology has shown that the mind best understands facts when they are woven into a conceptual fabric, such as a narrative, mental map, or intuitive theory. Disconnected facts in the mind are like unlinked pages on the Web: They might as well not exist.

—Steven Pinker

To try and remove the confusion I may have created in previous paragraphs, I'd like to note here that humans do need to learn to detach. It is attachment to an item, thing, or person that causes us so much pain, worry, and stress. We need to learn to detach to enjoy each day as it comes with a positive mind. We should not allow our expectations to cloud our vision by being excessively concerned about others. Such concerns bombard our logical and illogical thoughts, creating a web of unfinished business, even when there is no business. This has the potential to stop us from achieving a greater inner peace and especially a good night's sleep.

I'm sure many of you are thinking, 'That's easier said than done,' as another thought jumps into your mind about what someone has said or how we feel we need to be more considerate towards others. Or maybe we're angry and want to tell someone how they're making our lives a living hell. Now I shall say something that many don't want to hear. The most important thing in this life is not your mother, father, sister, brothers, friends, or even your children. The most important thing in this life is you and your personal well-being.

Connecting with others is a fundamental part of being a human; we need connection, but it must be controlled connection. If we cannot escape the grip of another, even when alone, we should ask, 'Is that grip taking away our ability to think, sleep, and live without an overwhelming feeling of guilt?'

Guilt is a wasted emotion, where we encounter remorse, reproach ourselves, and allow our conscience to dictate terms without any consideration or negotiation. Life is too short to continually worry about what another may think, has done, or may do.

Memories are thoughts that arise. They're not realities. Only when you believe that they are real, then they have the power over you. But when you realize it's just another thought arising about the past, then you can have a spacious relationship with that thought. The thought no longer has you in its grip.

—Eckhart Tolle

Not being gripped by thought or thinking too much about anything, I suddenly had a refreshing thought: Perhaps, in my lifetime, it might be possible for the world's population to finally grasp that all people, genders, and cultures are important and that we should work together to ensure all beliefs, values, and cultures are respected without prejudice. Why would I have such an impossible dream, especially considering how currently people, countries, and neighbours are continually fighting each other?

I could offer an answer on why people fight. However, I shall not bother, as I don't want to justify the horrors of war, terrorism, or domestic violence. Instead, my mind drifts to a pleasurable Friday when I took time out from my normal work routine to attend a one-day workshop that allowed me to learn more about gender diversity. I was pleased it was not about increasing the numbers to make the percentages look better, as I have always believed this is incorrect; people should be employed on merit.

The workshop was introduced as gender intelligence, which I liked, as it removed the concept of the need to employ a set amount of this, that, and the other to ensure a workforce is diverse and includes men and women. What made it even more interesting for me was that this was a company initiative.

This, in my mind, is a good initiative, especially as our company operates in over forty-eight countries, making it global, multicultural, and diverse without thought or reason. It makes business sense to harness all this diversity. It's a win-win situation. The company gets the best from our employees, and the employees get the best from the company.

Any business that does not look at the full potential of their people shall always be losing out to those that encourage, welcome, and promote creativity from all staff, no matter their position, gender, nationality, or creed. Gender intelligence, in my view, is the evolution of fair play for all without exception. The globalisation of company assets and products has already taught companies that having people from diverse backgrounds can introduce an array of new ideas and creativity.

However, one should also be a realist. Many industries are male-dominated and fail to attract some of the brightest minds due to longstanding perceptions and stereotypes. Due to the nature of the work or the mind-set of those that work within those industries, women are not attracted, and in some cases not invited, to these industries. That does not offer a fair go for all.

Therefore, these male-dominant industries are losing the richness of gender diversity and intelligence. In my opinion, the oil, gas, and construction industries need to look at how they can open their doors and, moreover, their minds. This is to attract the best talent from both genders through a mind-set change and, where necessary, an actual change to ensure equal opportunities are being offered. This will remove single-gender dominance in any industry, as this is not promoting gender intelligence and instead promotes prejudice and chauvinism.

I love those who can smile in trouble, who can gather strength from distress, and grow brave by reflection. 'Tis the business of little minds to shrink, but they whose heart is firm, and whose conscience approves their conduct, will pursue their principles unto death.

—**Leonardo da Vinci**

To close, and before moving from anobody to a somebody, please take time to read Leonardo da Vinci's quote again. Take heed in his words, especially the part that says, 'Tis the business of little minds to shrink'. Shrinking should only happen to woollens that are incorrectly washed, never to a person.

CHAPTER 14

Calling the Souls

Non-violence leads to the highest ethics, which is the goal of all evolution. Until we stop harming all other living beings, we are still savages.

—Thomas A. Edison

In the previous chapter, which was titled 'Nobody', I tried to identify that we are all someone. But many people have left this life, leaving their family and friends to wonder where they've gone. Some are never found, and many more (over centuries of war and violence) have been buried in unmarked graves.

This chapter is titled 'Calling the Souls', and I hope you'll enjoy what I've written about a place that I recently visited. It is called Lao Cai, meaning the Temple of Our Ladies, which is located on the Vietnam side of the border crossing between Vietnam and China.

As I have my photo taken, smiling with friends, I think of how forgiving people can be over the losses and heartaches they have suffered due to pointless wars. From about a few metres away, I can hear chants coming from within a temple. I'm told this is the Temple for Our Ladies, which was built between 1847 and 1883 on the fork of the river that separates Vietnam from China and where a bridge now stands to join the two countries.

As well all know, both these countries have a rich historical background. However, there are some parts of history that are rarely discussed by either government. Case in point is the war that began between Vietnam and China in 1979, known as the Sino-Vietnamese war. The conflict continued until 1988, peaking between 1984 and 1985. These wars happened but are never discussed between these two very proud countries.

Why do neighbours sometimes want to kill each other? Was it just a bunch of high-spirited soldiers shooting at each other without any concept of the consequences? Was it a power play by China, which was trying to show its might? Or was it simply a land grabbing exercise? What is known is that the mighty Chinese army did not expect their strength to be challenged and, I would even say, beaten. The Chinese never considered how battle-hardened the Vietnamese troops were, as compared to their own. These hostilities between two communist groups would have been seen by the West as the beginning of the end of a strong communist pact. They may have hoped that these localised battles would erupt into a full-fledged war, where one country would be destroyed and the other weakened.

As my imagination became overwhelmed with an effort to grasp how two countries with such rich histories and a common ancestry could kill each other, my solitude and inner thoughts were abruptly interrupted. Still, chants and mystic music, which sounded very spiritual, continued to emanate from the temple. I thought it was monks carrying out their daily rituals, but as I moved closer, I saw many people sitting.

A person dressed in white was sitting in the centre of the small temple facing the shrine. It appeared he was deep in thought and offering prayers. His clothing and the way the people who surrounded him followed his every word and action made me understand that this was something special. His clothes and headdress made me think of death. The only explanation I can offer for this is that white is usually worn at funerals. However, the only person wearing white was the person in the middle.

As I got closer, the chants and music got louder. I felt my own body vibrate from within, and that made me stop, as the feeling coming from the temple was spine-chilling. My intuition stopped me from entering the temple. I had goose pimples, and the hairs on the back of my neck stood up.

Spiritual relationship is far more precious than physical. Physical relationship divorced from spiritual is body without soul.

—Mahatma Gandhi

I'll explore my feelings at that moment later, but for now, I'll write about what I saw. As I was approaching, a young man entered and sat.

While this was happening, I was getting closer, and my emotions and feelings were changing. And as I decided not to enter, I heard screams.

The young man I had observed entering just a few minutes before was now being carried outside by a group of people. Initially, I thought he had collapsed and they were taking him outside to get some air. But as more people tried to support him, he began to convulse. My western mind instantly thought he was having some type of fit as he twitched and stiffened. He was murmuring and trying to call out something, but the voice I heard did not seem to be his. This may sound strange, as I had never met him or spoken to him. But I was sure that the voice that was coming out of his mouth was not his. He was a young man, and the voice was cold. It was a voice of suffering. The cries seemed to echo across the cobblestoned courtyard.

I walked away slowly, deep in thought, as I searched my memory to clearly understand what had just happened. The young man's cries had been the sounds of something trying to connect, to reach out. Once I was away from there, I asked Mr Nguyen, my Vietnamese friend, what all that was about. He explained that the people in the temple were attending a local ritual which tried to connect people with their relatives that had passed away. They wanted to communicate with their loved ones who had passed, needing to know they were safe on the other side. My friend said he didn't believe in this kind of stuff, and so I listened to his words without saying anything. Walking away on my own, I said nothing, but I felt exhausted, tired, and drained of energy.

I could have attributed the exhaustion I felt at that moment to having slept poorly the night before. That would have been the logical and acceptable explanation. So as I kept walking, I focused on the greenery and listened to the sounds of people. Then I heard what I needed to hear: the laughter of a child and the loving voice of a mother. The language was clear; it was the language of love. They were playing together without a care in the world. I stood and became absorbed in this beautiful scene for a few seconds, feeling my body being recharged with the most beautiful feeling. I instantly relaxed, just standing in a world of my own, until my friend brought me back to Earth, saying, 'You look very relaxed, Mr John.'

This is one of those special moments where I regained my inner strength not by popping pills or sleeping for eight hours but by allowing all of the positives things that surrounded me to enter my world. I didn't allow any negative external forces to interrupt me. Nor did I try to negotiate, justify, or analyse the beauty of the source of the free-flowing positive energy. I merely collected the laughter of a stranger, the sounds of nature, and the sensations of the environment. This is my time, a special time, which I try and get every day. I basically take thirty minutes (at least) each day to tune myself into a single positive vibe. Once I've tuned in, I can multiply this positive vibe until I am one with myself. And I find the internal batteries of life become magically and fully charged.

We need to lift our hope and fill our hearts with positive thoughts. Once this is understood by the masses, dictators shall be overthrown and democracy shall cease to be wanted, as the individualist attitudes that survive within a Western democracy shall no longer be tolerated.

Please do not get me wrong. I will always promote individualism, where a person can speak freely and love whom they wish without prejudice or persecution, as long as their individualism does not harm others or remove their ability to hold and speak openly about their own beliefs, thoughts, and choices. We must be individuals, but individuals who understand we need to connect and not stand alone. Alone, we shall perish. Strength is gained from joining hands in a marriage of diversity in it truest form, including black, white, yellow, green, and all the colours of the rainbow as well as all genders and nationalities, where the language of the world is one of peace.

New Age values are conscious evolution, a non-sectarian society, a non-military culture, global sharing, healing the environment, sustainable economies, self-determination, social justice, economic empowerment of the poor, love, compassion in action, going beyond religious fundamentalism, going beyond nationalism-extreme nationalism, culture.

—Deepak Chopra

Chapter 15 will explore and challenge an Einstein view on absolute truth. Do not get worried; I am not going to write a thesis on relativity or explain how light curves. I shall give you a view of reason from another viewpoint, Mr John's viewpoint. But before you turn the page, take thirty minutes to reenergise your internal batteries. Take thirty minutes to do something you want to do, something you do not need to do but want to do because it will make you feel good. See you in thirty minutes.

CHAPTER 15

Reasoning

Some truths fit into a category of 'definitely assured knowledge' that was 'grounded in reason itself.'

—Einstein

Who am I to challenge the most celebrated brain on this planet? But I'm sure he would be more than willing to accept that rules and theories need to be challenged. Let's consider the term 'definitely assured knowledge'. It is posed to convince us that we cannot argue with the known, as 'definitely' means without question and beyond doubt. However, can we be certain what is known today will definitely be the same tomorrow? Assured knowledge is based on what is known today, and yet we shall never truly understand what will happen tomorrow. I can say with certainty that science has continually challenged the theories and facts of the past, to a point that many of those facts and theories are no longer accepted. However, the learned few would have argued that the facts and theories would have been grounded in the reasons of the day, which would have been considered sound and unquestionable. That is the wonder of the human race and especially people like Einstein, those special individuals who challenged the establishments and norms of their time.

With this in mind, and expanding on my theory that the quotation offered as the opening of this chapter isn't quite correct, I would argue that people shall always believe in what is being said or printed. They may even say it is the truth. But I shall say do not be fooled, especially when considering how people try and influence us by saying such things as 'it's grounded in reason.' One would consider such a statement as meaning the thing can be substantiated. But people, being people, would instantly consider they are capable of consciously making sense of things. However, this is flawed, as reason is based on an individual's knowledge, experience, and education. Therefore, to ensure that others accept what I am saying, I need to convince them that what I consider as fact is indeed a fact. This is done by applying logic and grounding my arguments on reason, to verify what I am saying is factual.

Conversely, the facts posed are based on what is known at that time, with the data available. But what if our tools to measure the data are changed and upgraded, giving us new evidence? This might make what we said in the past incorrect. Therefore, to ensure we are still respected and don't lose our reputations, we would have to offer the new fact and theories in such a manner that people can see the benefits.

Feeding the one thing all humans have, curiosity, will give us the opportunity to spread the new facts and theories, as our newfound knowledge, if not listened to, may expose people and reduce further advancements.

Therefore, we shall need to convince all the people again that what we said is 'definitely assured knowledge' that was 'grounded in reason itself.' So the process shall need to start all over again. Except to gain the trust of others, I would need to be able to justify that what I said in the past was and is still reasonable and factual. Otherwise, others would not accept what we are proposing now.

'Excellent,' we may think, but it's not that easy, as people in general don't like change. So how can I influence others without threatening them? I need to get the masses to buy in, follow, and generalise. People like to follow, especially if we can convince them it is the norm.

Therefore, I shall need to create something that is believed, something that will protect them and give them hope for a better life, even after this life. Once I have created this belief, and it is embedded in their minds as good, I now have the power to manipulate millions.

At this point I would like to ask two questions:

- Is history real, or is it composed of lies?
- Can I say that the text of all religions are factual, or are they made up?

Using the principle that certain truths can only be discovered by reason alone, I could question both of the points above. History is written by the winners and often changes to suit the views of the government in power, even if this means not telling the whole truth and nothing but the truth. Religion is so powerful that the leaders of these religious groups can get their followers to do things without hesitation or question. However, stories that are being told and believed are not grounded in reason. They are believed for no other reason than the fact that people have been conditioned to believe. Call it blind faith, if you will.

I am sure many of these stories are based on historical events. And over time, they have been discussed and rewritten to record the same events with different words to suit the language of the day. I will even say that the first records written were considered truthful accounts. The first storytellers were convinced that what was written was the truth. However, as time passed, maybe the initial words were interpreted several times to emphasise or remove a specific point, to suit the current times.

The question that crosses my mind now is: Were these factual accounts or a biased view gathered by those who wanted to control others by offering them hope? David Hume (1711–1776) was sceptical about any knowledge other than what could be directly perceived by the senses. I offer the following as a simple explanation. David Hume was a Scottish philosopher born in 1711 in Edinburgh, Scotland. Hume is famous for continuing the tradition of empiricism, started by Locke and followed by Berkeley, which sees knowledge as coming originally from sense experience. Hume differs from these philosophers, however, in that he remains sceptical about what causes our perceptions of things.

While Locke assumes there is a material substance which causes our perceptions, and Berkeley presents the radical thesis that our perceptions originate in the mind of God, Hume refuses to make either assumption. His scepticism leads him to question whether there really are causes and effects or if our concept of causality is merely the result of the mind's practical nature (*An Enquiry Concerning Human Understanding*).

Considering the tradition of empiricism and thinking out loud about the questions above, I would say here that blind faith is just that: blind faith? However, this is just my opinion.

To those who believe their faiths are real and accept the stories given as evidence of why they need to follow without questioning, I only have one thing to say: 'Good on you.' I shall never accept all that is said is an absolute truth. My scepticism is high, especially as I watch people kill each other due to blind faith that is not grounded by reason.

I shall let you ponder that. If you can say without a hint of doubt that all that was written, interpreted, and repeated is true, excellent. If not, do not lose your faith or your beliefs. Just understand why you choose to believe it and keep your faith. I would say that in most instances, it is your need to belong, as belonging gives us hope.

I may sound cynical, which I am, when it comes to blind faith or accepting what is said as being the truth and nothing but the truth. But one should always question, as to follow without understanding why reduces us to mindless individuals. In my opinion, this is a waste, as we are born with a brain that is so powerful if used properly. So please continue to learn, explore, and observe what is happening around you.

However, be mindful. Our brains can be confused, even when we have witnessed and observed a specific thing. Are we 100 per cent sure of what we have witnessed and observed? Do we always see and hear things clearly? Are our senses so flawless that we can say without doubt that we saw and heard what we thought? Many a witness in cross-examinations have been proven wrong.

My knowledge and experiences are directly related to what I have been exposed to, learnt, and gained through living each and every moment. These are my building blocks, the foundation of my perception. Therefore, I cannot say with 100 per cent certainty that my perceptions will be the same as those of others. I cannot even say with certainty that what I perceive is correct. However, I do not feel confused, as I accept that I only know what I know and others may know more or less, due to their age, experiences, and education levels. When I talk about education I do not solely refer to what is learnt in schools or university, as this can be biased, depending on which country you are educated in.

When I talk about education, I mean all things learnt from every moment you've experienced since birth. This is the education of life. Formal education is just a means to share a structured curriculum that is considered by those in power as important to give our young people the skills to advance and become useful adults.

Nevertheless, formal education is more about identifying different levels of ability. It has a grading system that can identify the talented few while offering limited support for the people who struggle. Furthermore, one should not forget how the school system from those very first days introduces competition, where students have to strive to be the best to ensure they are selected to advance. Please do not get me wrong: healthy competition is good, as it makes an individual grow and understand. We have to work and sometimes work very hard to gain success.

I am not sure authorities will argue they are thinking of what is best for individuals. But in most circumstances I would say that they are thinking of how they can control and stop chaos. Therefore, they introduce rules, systems, and processes, and moreover, they manipulate the truth by conditioning the masses to believe and respect.

Blind Respect for authority is the greatest enemy of truth.

—Jost Winteler

In my opinion, blind respect for anything or anyone is akin to being disrespectful to yourself. We were given a brain and the ability to think freely. This ability allows us to create, invent, and, better still, explore all that has not been explored before. With our minds, we can search and discover for new things that will ensure a brighter future for all mankind.

However, this will require strength. Respected rules, theories, and laws will need to be challenged and possibly changed, thereby exposing yourself and others to ridicule. The learned few who hold power to manipulate the masses will not want the status quo changed, as this will remove their ability to control.

To explore my thoughts further and test my opinions, I asked a friend to read what I had written. As I have said, I only know what I know, and this knowledge has been gained over many years of living, learning, and, more importantly, listening. I have strong opinions, but I accept others may know more. This is what my friend said:

The very first knowledge given to mankind was about the apple tree. He warned Adam and Eve not to eat fruit from that tree. The rest, as you know, is history. He and only He can give knowledge to whomever He chooses: Adam, Moses, Josef, David, Solomon, Jesus, Muhammad, etc.

Giving knowledge and giving direction to the Right Path are two different things. Again, the Master has the absolute right to give to whomever he wishes to give to, one or the other, or both. This is His universal and divine secret since the creation of the universe. For example: Sir Isaac Newton was given the knowledge of the falling apple and its relationship with the law of gravity. So, he became famous for that discovery. But what he failed to ask was, who made the apple and cause the apple to fall back to Earth?

Newton read the Bible well, but he failed to explore the Quran, the final book of prophecy and the history of the universe, past, present, and future. Hence, Newton failed to see the true path of the absolute creator of the Universe, the creator of mankind. Maybe he saw it at some point, but he ignored it for some reason.

Why did God not give him those insights? This I cannot answer, because it is His secret. Human beings have secrets. So, obviously, God has His own secrets too. He can do whatever He wishes, and He has his own reasoning. That is part of His holy secret and His absolute divine power. His presence is all around us, at all times.

My apologies if all this sounds disturbing to you. Using my knowledge of the '5 Why Analysis' or rather 5Whos, it will all eventually lead to one and only one answer, i.e., God, the Creator and Owner of the universe.

But above all, I do respect what other people believe or perceive about the universe and reasoning.

Nature and Natures laws lay hid in night: God said, let Newton be! And all was light.

—Alexander Pope

I have read this a few times and loved that my friend would take the time to read my words, offer his thoughts, and then allow me to use his words as part of this chapter.

There are many of philosophers, scientists, and billions of others who do believe in divine intervention. They believe in God, so maybe they do not need to look further than the holy books of their chosen religion, as they believe the absolute truth is written within these books. They also have faith in divine intervention, which is God causing something good to happen or God preventing something bad from happening. However, others, such as atheists, agnostics, and deists, will always find alternate explanations for even the most miraculous of events, even those that on occasion the greatest minds cannot fathom.

I'd like to think there is a God, but the God I'm talking about is the one that loves all living and dead things without discrimination, prejudice, or distinction. This God will not intervene, stop events, or take sides on this Earth, as the visitors of this land, being humans, animals, plants, and all those other living things, are just temporary citizens. We are all being allowed some time to explore. Maybe one day we shall have a lightbulb moment and realise that there are things that God did not give us, such as hatred, greed, jealousy, discrimination, prejudice, bigotry, lust, and the need to control others. I could fill pages upon pages with the things that I feel we humans have created, because we can. We are free-thinking individuals that are allowed to explore, discover, and evolve. Our intellect is also growing. We are continually being exposed to new things, making our brains work more. I honestly think most humans can use 100 per cent of their brain, or I should say 100 per cent of the parts of the brain that have stored data and are connected and plugged in.

However, another human trait is laziness, or offering excuses as to why we cannot do something even before trying. Once we start to open ourselves to the world and remove the shackles of myth and the unknown, we shall start to learn new things, and our incredible brain shall keep up. That is, if we believe and strive without discrimination, prejudice, or distinction.

There is so much more we will be able to do in the future, if we open up and stop restricting ourselves by being controlled by myths and stories of the past, or worse, by people, associations, and organisations of the present.

You might be thinking, *John, what you're suggesting may well create chaos.* If this thought has indeed crossed your mind, please don't think that I'm suggesting such things. I am sorry to say that I think I do not *need* to create chaos. I think many parts of the world, if not all the world, are already in chaos. We see disorder, confusion, and disarray appearing across the world, and much is due to religion, not God. We cannot blame anything that is occurring on this planet to God; it is all man-made. And to all the preachers, clerics, dictators, tyrants, and people who try and control through violence or manipulation: Get a life! Stop using others to promote your lies and hatred! I was thinking about using the word 'ignorance', but these manipulators are not ignorant. They are smart, as they can get others to do what they cannot or will not do.

People, in general, are good and kind; they like to live in peace. Maybe that's why we do not live forever and we say, 'Rest in Peace,' when someone passes away. Due to the chaos of the world, we would think there was something wrong if we didn't hear of atrocities, terrorist attacks, or an individual gone crazy.

I would even go as far as saying that, sadly, people are now becoming immune to bad news, and in some cases it is becoming the norm. I have always disagreed with how we consider something as normal. Just because many people are doing it or believe in it does not make it good or normal.

Love thy neighbour as you love yourself. Whoops! I just had a thought as to why these radicals, extremists, and die-hard nutters want to kill, maim, mutilate, and torture others. They do not love themselves. Therefore they do not know how to live and forgive others. I do not feel sorry for these individuals or groups. I pity them, as they hide behind their radical views or self-pity by blaming everything, apart from themselves. Reality and truth are not within their grasps.

Compassion and tolerance are not a sign of weakness, but a sign of strength.

—Dalai Lama

I can show compassion and tolerance, and I can forgive. Therefore, this must mean I have inner strength. What is sometimes hard is to forget, and this is the problem we humans face. We continually live in the past, not allowing ourselves or, worse, our young to see the future. We condition them to believe as we believe, instead of allowing them to be free to believe in what they want.

Here, I should thank my mother, as she did allow me to be a free spirit. Even though she had a sharp tongue and quick hand, she never told me I had to believe in anything apart from myself.

With this in mind, I do like reading about ancient philosophers, such as Socrates, as I like the concept of introducing a process of questions and answers. You get a person to put his point, and then you continually ask questions to try and raise doubt in the person's thoughts or ideas. We seek to expose the thought to contradiction. However, the beauty of this was, Socrates then guided us to arrive at a solid conclusion. Perry Mason, now I know where you learnt to cross-examine. Don't forget that Socrates was born over 2,400 years ago. I should also mention Plato, or the one Greek philosopher that I would say most are familiar with, Aristotle, who travelled to Athens to learn in the institution founded by Socrates and taught by Plato. What an incredible place!

I liked how he wrote about logic, nature, psychology, ethics, politics, and art. In fact, Aristotle had a view on all things that were known or unknown. He was credited with developing deductive reasoning. Sounds like Sherlock Holmes may have studied Aristotle's methods!

Another great philosopher that most people would know is Master Kong Qiu, better-known as Confucius. Most people today would say democracy was the invention of the Greeks and a Western idea. But Confucius is known for challenging governments of the East. He believed a good government was one that ruled on rites and the people's natural morality, rather than by using bribery, coercion, or manipulation. This sounds obvious to us, as it is what the Western world prides itself on, and many now fight for this magical thing called democracy. But isn't this what the Greeks argued for and developed, a system of rule by people based on the concept that the people's morality is in charge? However, this will only work once the people of the world agree on what is right and wrong or what constitutes good or bad behaviour.

OK, enough of the past. Let's consider the person whom many who have studied philosophy would consider the father of modern philosophy. This would be Rene Descartes, who lived between 1596 and 1650. He is known for creating analytical geometry and I am sure may have given quite a few of us headaches, as it is still taught in schools today. Analytical geometry is the study of geometry using algebra and the Cartesian coordinate system.

However, not to turn you off, Descartes also discovered the law of refraction and reflection. He also invented the superscript notation still used today to indicate the powers of exponents. Now you may be scratching your head. To end my rant on Descartes, I'd like to remind you that he created exponents to save you from writing out lots of multiples, like: $8^2 = 8 \times 8 = 64$. Ah, I hear you say. And the non-mathematical types may be thinking, *whatever.*

However, as you know if you have read any of my books, I like quotations, and one of his famous quotations is, 'I think, therefore I am.'

This statement must be understood as he wanted it to be understood. It is not meant to prove the existence of one's body. Quite the opposite, it is meant to prove the existence of one's mind. As I have repeatedly stated over several years, even before reading or studying philosophy, a person's strength is not made up of his or her body size or muscle mass. It consists of the person's ability to think freely, challenge, and continually ask why.

Descartes rejected perception as unreliable. Remember, our perception is made up by our experiences, observations, and information that we have gathered over time. Therefore, it may be limited due to our education, culture, and customs or the limitations placed on us due to where we live or what others in power allows us to learn or believe. He considered deduction the only reliable method for examining, proving, and disproving anything.

Ah, now we are aligned. My friend would be happy too, as he did not say God was a myth. In fact, he also adhered to the ontological argument for the existence of a God, stating that because God is benevolent, Descartes can have some faith in the account of reality his senses provided him. God has provided him with a working mind and a sensory system that does not desire to deceive him.

I am not disagreeing with what Descartes believed. However, times passed also required philosophers and scientists to step lightly when it came to writing new ideas and theories or challenging religious thoughts and beliefs. A great example of this was Galileo's punishment, handed down in 1633 by the Catholic church. This church tried and found many an innocent person guilty, all because they went against what they said was the absolute truth. Why was Galileo persecuted? Because he wrote that the earth revolves around the sun, which was deemed heretical by the Catholic church. And why did the church think this? Because Galileo provided a different view from what was written within the holy and divine scriptures. So Pope Urban VIII's loyal team ruled that Galileo was spreading false doctrines that were contrary to the holy and divine scriptures, as well as what the church and its respected, learned peoples were saying and preaching.

That the sun moved around the earth was an absolute fact of scripture that could not be disputed. This was despite the fact that scientists had known for centuries that the Earth was not the centre of the universe.

The church pronounced, judged, and declared that Galileo was guilty. He spent the rest of his life under house arrest. It took more than three hundred years for the church to admit that Galileo was right and to clear his name of heresy. This is not an attack on the Catholic church or any other religious group. But many people have been put to death and are still being persecuted due to words in holy books and how those words are being interpreted and used to spread fear, terror, and control.

I'm sure that even the great Descartes was careful in what he wrote. Maybe he withheld his own views and excluded anything unorthodox from his published writing. But this did not save his work from being added to the Roman Catholic index of prohibited books. I am sure the list would be a wonderful read and also include any and all writing that may have offered a different view than or challenged those words that have been used to control billions of believers.

However, I shall say without referencing a book or Google that I think much of the past is no more than a few well-written stories. True or not true, I shall not debate. I will even add that I am sure the great prophets were real people and they led their people with the hope of salvation. This took vision and unselfish love. It was the people who spoke after these prophets had left this Earth who created, in my view, the stories, myths, and in part superstitions. Why? That I cannot answer with certainty. All I can say is that the stories, myths, and superstitions still hold billions of people to this day, due to hope and the belief of a better life after this one or the fear of going to Hell.

I can even state that many of these superstitions would contradict natural science. However, natural science is a branch of science concerned with the description, prediction, and understanding of natural phenomena, based on observational and empirical evidence. I'm sure Einstein would say that definitely assured knowledge was grounded in reason itself.

But – and there is always a but – even science, research, and the best minds in town cannot explain all that has occurred and may occur. Miracles do happen, and even the church and religious groups accept that much of the past was just superstition and that natural science, and science in general, have a place. But I say again, miracles do happen.

I do think there is a higher power that understands more than we humans do. Many will say this is God, and I am happy that people do believe in God. But I am not prejudiced against those who do not believe. However, I have read more than once that God was said to be the Great Designer, and I like this. I have also read that we were made in the image of God. This I cannot accept, as I drink my coffee looking at all the different images walking past.

I will conclude that human behaviour might be instinctive or driven by bodily appetites and passion, like that of other animals. But our ability to reason is special, providing an insight into rational truth. We may not be right all the time, and yes, we make mistakes. But that is the beauty of being human, as imperfection is perfection. Maybe I should remove my sceptical hat and allow myself to just accept that the Great Designer is out there watching over us, not to interfere but just to see how long it will take for us to understand what we have and the powers that are trapped within our minds.

If only we would stop fighting each other and learn to accept it is our prejudices that limit our success. If we can remove these prejudices and discriminations and become more tolerant towards each other, our rational insight may extend much further. This is where we accept and believe in ourselves, whereby we remove the needs for false hope and being scared of old superstitions.

God has given us faculties suitable for our position in the world, as creatures intermediate between animals and angels. And though our reason might be fallible and limited, it above all is what elevates us above the beast.

—Peter Millican

CHAPTER 16

I Am a Writer, So Must I Be Able to Write and Create?

Every human being has hundreds of separate people living under his skin. The talent of a writer is his ability to give them their separate names, identities, personalities and have them relate to other characters living with him.

—Mel Brooks

I'm thinking of writing a silly story, something that will make people feel joy, reflect, and, with luck, get an emotional response that will make them feel good. But nothing is happening. No words are forming. Think silly? What is silly? How do I write about something silly? I'm thinking. Ah, I've got it. Governments! I could write about world leaders, the false promises they make, and the policies they enforce that are supposedly good' for us. Ha ha! Now that's a silly thought! I laugh out loud as I think of the unrighteous – whoops, I meant to say righteous – few who hold positions of power and try to govern. To say that they govern would be obviously false when we look at the world today. Now that was a silly thought, but not a silly story, even though I'm sure there are many silly and funny stories about governments and individual politicians. As I read the newspaper or, better still, read between the lines of what the so-called leaders are saying, I note that there seem to be many silly stories on these pages, but they are not my stories. What can I write about? How can I create or find a story from nothing?

Then, I have a lightbulb moment. Writers never have a blank sheet of paper. They may lack the words to write, but all around them, there is a story. However, to capture those stories, they need to be patient, listen, see, hear, touch, and feel all that is evolving within their sphere. Every moment captures all the riches that are spinning in the World Wide Web, as a spider captures its prey.

However, this can only be done if we learn to keep our mouths shut and our senses alert, where a mega production could be made. Action! Cut! Roll! All this activity is occurring in the most magical film set ever created, your mind. It's a truly wonderful place, with your very own movie theatre that filters, compresses, and stores away beautiful memories until you decide to access those files once again and share them with others.

One must consider all points of view, without prejudice or scepticism. Sure, this is easy to write, but it's hard to do. Still, life is good, which is something I say repeatedly. What I usually don't add to that is: The meaning of life, to me, is accepting life as I live it, including every moment and all of it. Love, hatred, happiness, and suffering are all part of the meaning of life.

However, this is a challenge, as humans are guided by preconceived boundaries of what can and cannot be done. Rules, conditions, and social norms are continually being enforced, from our childhood and throughout our lives. This restrictive process can remove the ability of many individuals to think freely. Maybe I'm wrong, but I don't believe that it is a sin to think and even dream. Daydreaming is when you consider what is possible and sometimes what may be considered impossible.

When I daydream, I breathe, closing my eyes to give my body and soul air while drifting in and out of reality. I can still do this while living a productive life and earning enough to support myself and others in my life. And the way I accept this life allows me to capture much more than I did in the past. I see beauty every day. I see pain and suffering most days. If this sentence has captured your attention, I would like to elaborate on it a little further, to explain the kinds of beauty, pain, and suffering that I see. The most beautiful things are those simple things, such as watching a family enjoy their time together, listening to birds sing, and seeing an elderly couple hold hands. The pain I see is the frustration on people's faces as they think they are failing, how others frown with contempt when someone makes a mistake, or how we humans lack patience and tolerance. This is what pains me most. I see suffering in everyday life, and I'm not talking about what I read. Instead, I'm talking about seeing homeless people sleeping on the sidewalk, elderly people wandering alone and counting the days before they die, and young people losing themselves in alcohol and drugs. However, I also see 'love all around,' a wonderful line from the memorable movie *Love Actually.* If you have not seen it, go out and buy it; it's a nice movie.

I often sit quietly, minding my own business, blending in with my surroundings. I am sure I am invisible to some, as they talk and expose their souls while explaining most wonderful tales. They're not aware that others can hear them. Maybe many others don't want to hear them but instead shut themselves off to the world and live only in their insulated world of rules, conditions, and the norm.

The world is a crazy, beautiful, ugly complicated place, and it keeps moving on from crisis to strangeness to beauty to weirdness to tragedy. The caravan keeps moving on and the job of the Longford writer or filmmaker or radio broadcaster is to stop – is to pause – and when the caravan goes away, that is when this stuff comes.

—David Remnick

Thinking of times gone bye, I recall a time when I went out west. I don't mean the Wild West, though maybe it can be considered that to some. I'm talking about a place called St George in Queensland, Australia, where I was invited to attend an outback wedding. When I got to St George, I realised that rain had not fallen there for years. The land was dry, while the sense of humour was even drier. This hot and fly-ridden place causes limited tolerance for us city folk. The flies do their best to enter every orifice we humans have, and all they do is eat, regurgitate, and eat again.

Oh to be a fly, flutter, flutter. Oh what I would be able to see and hear as a fly on the wall.

The wager is on. The bet is to see who has the strongest willpower to allow those larger than large, black-winged, poo-eating flies to land and walk where they wish, without lifting a hand to wave them away. So I stand tall, taking on the challenge and allowing them to land, climb, sit, and flutter around my face. The flies look for somewhere dark and warm, such as a hairy nostril, a moist eye, or a waxy ear. 'Willpower!' I hear myself say, as internally, I am screaming.

I look around at all those who have taken the bet and am pleased to see that they are all struggling. I even forget my own struggles as I focus on their facial expressions and their hands, gripping their trousers to stop their natural instinct of waving these germ-carrying insects away. Then, as some start to falter, the formal part of the wedding ceremony commences, and the celebrant speaks. Vows are said. Just as our friend is asked the million-dollar question, will he take bla bla bla as his lawfully-wedded wife, a fly decides to explore the inside of his open mouth, causing our friend to choke. His father says that must be an omen, in a louder-than-loud voice, which causes an instant moment of relief as everyone all around bursts into laughter. Our laughter seems to echo through the air, scaring the flies away – apart from the one that by now has been de-winged, swallowed, and left forever flightless.

I am, however, pleased to say that the marriage survived. The fly-swallowing groom has since pledged his life, heart, and soul to his wonderful and beautiful lady. They live, love, and forever smile thinking of that very special moment. Well, I really hope that Simon and his wife are still smiling and overwhelmingly happy, as I have not heard from him or seen him in over a decade. But due to the fly, I have never forgotten his wedding.

Your writing voice is the deepest possible reflection of who you are. The job of your voice is not to seduce or flatter or make well-shaped sentences. In your voice, your readers should be able to hear the contents of your mind, your heart, your soul.

—Meg Rosoff

I like the quotation above, and I feel it is a writer's ultimate goal to offer words that allow others to escape, while sitting safely in their armchairs or wherever they may like to read. As a writer, I often ask myself questions, and it is these questions that I write about. My writing is where I share thoughts, ideas, and feelings and offer escapism, while not being scared to offer an opinion for others to read.

This is freedom, in words, thoughts, and acts. I offer those thoughts and words to you, the reader. When I cannot open one of those thousands of files in my brain, captured while living a wonderful life, I lock myself down and listen to music, any music. I truly try not to continually play a specific song or artist. I love being exposed to new songs and bands, and I love a large mix of genres.

In fact, currently my mind is drifting. I am listening to Beth Gibson. Her voice and lyrics are tugging and pulling at my inner emotions, and I think of a book I recently read: *Man's Search for Meaning,* by Viktor E. Frankl.

I will not say what he wrote about, but I will say this: it is a must-read book, as his words come alive on every page. I could connect to what he was saying, and this connection allowed me to be emotionally attached to all his experiences. So when he spoke of suffering, pain, love, and the meaning of life, he opened my mind. I allowed him in, so our souls could entwine, as I shut my eyes and wondered. Do I have his strength? Would I have been able to survive? What I do know that his words have touched my heart and given me even greater optimism. Perhaps I can now live the rest of my life always thinking that my glass is half full and sometimes having to give, as my glass of life is overflowing.

I shall share a single statement that is recorded within his book. The reason I like it is that it made me smile. 'I recommend that the Statue of Liberty on the east coast be supplemented by a Statue of Responsibility on the west coast.'

I could write a lot here about what that statement meant to me, but I shall not. Instead, I shall offer the following few paragraphs, to give you a view of my position on life and the meaning of life to me.

I have a tattoo on by back that says 'independence, freedom and happiness'. After reading those words, I thought I might need to visit the tattoo shop and have a few other words added. Maybe I should add ' responsibility and accountability'. The people of the world demand fair play, and most today desire democracy, which I am sure they believe will give them freedom. I have always promoted freedom, independence, and happiness, and I believe they are every person's right. However, to achieve this, individuals must understand they need to be held responsible and accountable for their actions, or lack of actions, and stop looking for excuses or an easy road to gain individualism with the hope of freedom.

My view of freedom is the ability decide on the life I want and live that life with the understanding that I am responsible for my actions and lack of actions. I should and shall be held accountable by others and myself for whatever I do or do not do.

However, let's be careful here. You can only be held responsible and accountable for things within your control or sphere of influence.

To die without finishing the book you were reading is an insult to the author.

—JRC

I just had a thought: I started this chapter by saying, 'Think of something silly,' and after reading the above few pages, I have gone from silly to serious. So I shall now say, I shall not be responsible or even accountable for what I may write. Whoops! Maybe I can be accountable, but never mind. I'm a man, and men can't multi-task. When I write, I put my writer's hat on. Normally, I don't think of such things, as I'm in my writer's box. A friend once explained to me the difference between men's and women's brains. Basically, he said, a man's brain is divided into boxes. In each box, we store different bits of information. For example, we have a box for our car, marriage, money, sex, and all those other things that we men have to think about, work with, play with, and dream about. None of these boxes touch each other.

After discussing it further and laughing even more, my friend then went onto YouTube and found a short clip from Mark Gungor called 'A Tale of Two Brains'. Mark is an author, speaker, and much more. He delivers extra-special marriage seminars, confronting both genders and giving very down-to-earth answers and insight into why those silly arguments over nothing occur.

After watching the small clip, we discussed how it appeared that women's brains are an open storage space, so all the sections can communicate freely. This is why, in our opinion, women can multi-task, where most men 'single task'. We men don't want to open too many of our boxes at once. They're mostly neatly stored away. However, in saying this, maybe we men only dream of multi-tasking. Or maybe not. We are happy doing one thing at a time. However, the bit I was most intrigued with was when he said that men have an empty box. This I could relate to. When my partner asks me what I'm thinking, I often say, 'Nothing.' She then looks at me strangely and says, 'You must be thinking of something,' to which I then answer with a blank face, 'Nothing. Why should I be thinking of something?' Little does she know that in that moment, I'm in my empty box.

This must be frustrating for most women. To do nothing, or worse, think of nothing, seems impossible and intolerable to them. Maybe that's why they hate watching their men sit and do nothing or fiddle with something for hours. Could it be jealousy on their part? Their brains are an open plan, in which we should discuss everything while browsing all in sight. It could be assumed that women's brains never turn off.

17 October 2014: Staring at the computer, I try to get words to appear on the page, but all I can think about is – how could I write a sentence if my brain had a word impediment, such as word stuttering? Is that how I should write 'stuttering', or should it be 'stu stu stutt

stutt stuttering'? Please excuse my meanness. I'm now thinking about plunging a knife into my heart or burning my tongue out using a hot iron. Silliness is writing what appears without vengeance or malice. It's black, white, yellow, blue, or green. I don't know what colour it is, or of it's female, male, transgender, or all the above. What am I exploring in the depths of my mind when I'm trying to write a new chapter?

What's the point of writing? Will people actually really read a book to learn, or to say, I have read a book'? I read, wrote, and repeated several times that to open a book without finishing it is an insult to the author. Well, that's my opinion anyway. I have bought hundreds of books, and I can say I have read them all. Some only took a few days, as I was interested in what I was reading, I needed to know about the topic, or I just loved what was written. These factors made it easy to read.

Reading others, I must be honest, was like having a toothache. Each page and every word written caused me pain, as my interest was not being captured. This is not written as a criticism to the authors, as I was not forced to buy their book. I bought it of my own free will. I normally buy my books based on their covers, and rarely do I read the back cover or listen to critics. I like to explore all words, thoughts, and opinions, so this exposes me to lots of new material. Sometimes, this includes a little bit of the not-so-good material. But again, this is just my opinion. I must be in my opinion box. Oh, I seem to be in that box a lot! I think I need to explore my empty box, where I can meditate in silence and gain balance through doing nothing. Get me out of my nothing box. No, keep me in my nothing box. Last night, I destroyed many of my hard-working brain cells by overindulging in wine, beer, and anything else that could flow while laughter was loud and the mood of the night was young. But today will be long and the mood … less than functional.

Everything that irritates us about others can lead us to an understanding of ourselves.

—Carl Jung

CHAPTER 17

Terrorism

If the mind is dominated by hatred, the best part of the brain which is used to judge right from wrong does not function properly

—Dalai Lama

In chapter 15, I questioned how grounded reason is used in conjunction with definitely-assured knowledge to ascertain what absolute truth is. However, the chapter also used the same theories to prove that what was said as part of history, or written within religious text, could not be accepted without question as definitely-assured knowledge. Now, I'm not trying to confuse or change your beliefs or values. Instead, I'm trying to get readers to open their eyes, ears, and all other senses, so we observe and absorb what is happening every day all around us. Is it fair for innocent people to be killed? Is it fair for the rich to become richer and the poor to become poorer? Is it fair that every year, people die of infections, illnesses, and cancers that, if treated early enough, could have been cured?

The World Health Organisation (WHO) reports that cancer is among the leading causes of death worldwide, with approximately 14 million new cases and 8.2 million cancer- related deaths in 2012. They predict the number of new cases is expected to rise by about 70 per cent over the next two decades. What scares me is not the increase in cancer cases but the number of people that could be saved by early diagnoses if governments were refocused and spent money on treating people, rather than on weapons to take lives. As people starve and die of diseases, on average, the global expenditure on weapons exceeds 1.7 trillion USD per year.

At a time when a deep economic recession is causing much turbulence in the civilian world... defence giants such as Boeing and EADS, or Finmeccanica and Northrop Grumman, are enjoying a reliable and growing revenue stream from countries eager to increase their military might.

Both geopolitical hostilities and domestic violence tend to flare up during downturns.

Shareholders and employees in the aerospace and defence industry are clearly the ones who benefit most from growing defence spending.

Defence companies, whose main task is to aid governments' efforts to defend or acquire territory, routinely highlight their capacity to contribute to economic growth and to provide employment.

Indeed, some $2.4 trillion (£1.5tr), or 4.4%, of the global economy 'is dependent on violence,' according to the Global Peace Index, referring to 'industries that create or manage violence' — or the defence industry.

Military might delivers geopolitical supremacy, but peace delivers economic prosperity and stability.

And that, the report insists, is what is good for business.

—Jorn Madslien, 'The Purchasing of Power of Peace', BBC, 3 June 2009

Should we just accept all that is being said? Or should we start to ask why or challenge what we are seeing, hearing, or being told by those in power? And I'm not just talking about governments here.

I would include here multinational companies, associations, and organisations. And we cannot forget the media, which deliver the messages of those in power to help the owners of publications to gain a larger market share.

Terrorism is happening and real, and sadly, in some parts of the world, it's becoming an everyday event. This is good business for those who supply arms and advice on military know-how.

News flash! Thursday, 2 April 2015. In Nairobi, Kenya, Somali militants burst into a university in eastern Kenya and kill 147 innocent students who dreamed and had ambitions to improve their lives. By the time this book is published, if it is published, this shocking news would be old and I'm sure forgotten by millions.

Because each and every day, we are bombarded with tales of horror, we're slowly becoming desensitised. The majority of the readers of these news articles aren't directly being affected, so their stories don't even make the front pages. And if they do, they don't hold the front page for long. Is it because people don't care? I would argue that people do care about other people, but we have become selective. We tend to block out things that could come to our country and affect each and every one of us. Maybe that's why the above story, about the 147 innocent people being killed, will be lost as yesterday's news. This type of attack is becoming everyday news.

This has reduced our ability to care, as the majority feel these everyday events are now beyond our control. So we block them out and say we have enough things to worry about in our own country. However, the people who may say this would, in general, be more than willing to send money or even volunteer to help a country or people that are affected by a natural disaster. Furthermore, natural disasters seem to hold the front page longer and attract greater coverage. Why is this? That's the first thing that I thought. Could it be our humanitarian side kicks in, and we feel our money and help will make a difference? Could it be we are not threatened or scared of retribution, remembering that terrorist groups thrive when others fear them?

Therefore, how do these terrorist groups get and keep our attention? Quite simple: by spreading fear. This feeds on human emotions, lifting our state of anger and hatred to the point that even the most reasonable, logical, and intellectual person starts to believe in part, if not all, of what is being said or told.

Einstein is known for being a pacifist and has openly said that people should not go to war. But his views did change as he witnessed in horror the changes that occurred within a country he loved. As Germany rearmed under the control of Adolf Hitler and started a hate campaign against Jews, it was reported that Einstein said: 'To prevent the greater evil, it is necessary that the less evil – the hated military – be accepted for the time being.'

Why? Because as humans, our inner instinct is to survey. Therefore, when we hear the T-word ('terror') or the other, bigger T-word ('terrorism'), we look for protection. This makes us more susceptible to the lies told by those in power. It doesn't matter which country, nationality, religion, or belief we may hold onto. We are now vulnerable to being manipulated and influenced to accept unlawful laws due to fear, anger, and in some cases ignorance. This can also cause us to change our beliefs and promote things that in the past would have never been considered, such as Einstein's views on conscription and military service. In his heart, he was still a pacifist, but he knew that to stand still and watch innocent people being persecuted was wrong. I will say here that I don't believe any person or government has any more rights than any other, but there is always a but! The 'but' in this instance is where a person, organisation, association, or government forces its beliefs on others, or when a group or governments is prejudiced and discriminates against a race, religion, gender, or sexuality.

I mean, what is racism? Racism is a projection of our own fears onto another person. What is sexism? It's our own vulnerability about our potency and masculinity projected as our need to subjugate another person, you know? Fascism, the same thing: People are trying to untidy our state, so I legislate as a way of controlling my environment.

—Gary Ross

Are the Ts coming? Do we all need to run, hide, and never openly say what we think, believe, or even like? Are we safe? Most countries now believe it is only a matter of time before they are attacked. More CCTV cameras are being installed in public spaces, more anti-terrorist task forces are being established, and more money is spent on defending their citizens from the threat of attack. However, many of the attacks are home-grown and not considered as terrorist acts. Call it what you wish, but any person who takes the life of an innocent person, or holds another prisoner against their will, is unleashing terror on another. Newspapers and governments use fear to stay in power and to gain votes.

Governments use the T-word to push defence budgets through, or to introduce new laws or change legislation, all under the mantle of creating a safer environment. This safer environment may also means the removal of basic human rights, where people can be imprisoned without being charged. People are investigated if they are rumoured to be associated with a known or even unknown group. I'm sure we the general public don't know all the groups or individuals that our government's protection agency have under scrutiny.

You may even, heaven forbid, disagree with the government of the day, and why shouldn't you disagree or ask questions? Is this not a democracy? Or maybe that's the problem. Governments are starting to realise that normal people, the voters, want answers, and those in power need to respond.

This will never do. A government that has to answer to the people? I can hear the old fraternity in government house saying, 'How can we govern? How can we rein them in?' And the professional bureaucrats offer the T-word. Maybe all that is being reported isn't 100 per cent the absolute truth. Could these fearful stories and headlines be fuelled by the same people that are trying to govern? Could it be that many of the governments that are protesting the loudest are two-faced and possibly having a two-way bet where their secret services offer advice, weapons, and funds to keep the T-word on the front page?

Could it be our governments are part of the T-word, maybe not directly but indirectly? And perhaps it suits them to fund the T-word indirectly, as to ensure they can control us and make the majority of us conformists?

However, even conformists can be troublesome, as the majority of people are conformists. We like being part of the crowd, we respond to informational influence, and currently, we are being fed lots of information and being made to view certain groups as difficult and even troublesome or evil. If I were to believe all that is being portrayed in the news, I would start to think Muslims in general are bad, as this is the general perception being portrayed. I will say here, I disagree: 23 per cent of the world's population are Muslims. I have never met a bad one or one who has treated me unfairly or unkindly, and I live in a Muslim country and have visited others.

The radical misfits who are creating fear and terror across the world are not your everyday hard-working Muslims, Christians, Buddhists, or any other particular group. They are people who lack the courage to open their hearts and minds to others' views, maybe because they're scared and insecure in their own beliefs and opinions. However, I am fearful that many people don't see the difference and consider all Muslims as radical misfits, which they are not. Maybe this is another issue we are being influenced to believe: To be a terrorist, you must have certain religious beliefs. This not true. Let's be honest. All religious groups have had radical individuals and breakaway groups, and that would include Christianity, Islam, Hinduism, Buddhism, Sikhism, Judaism, and I am sure the others too. Sadly, these misguided misfits have killed, maimed, and terrorised innocent people, all under the pretence that they are following the path of the righteous. What a load of rubbish! As far as I know, none of the great prophets talked of hatred or murder and never condoned suicide. Maybe I am wrong, but I thought Muhammad, Jesus, Buddha, and Moses promoted love, forgiveness, and acceptance.

What drives people to kill and maim each other so savagely, Einstein asked. 'I think it is the sexual character of the male that leads to such wild explosions':

—Einstein

I would agree with Einstein's perception that the humans have a built-in trait, such as fight or flight, which since man was born has been used to protect humankind. But look at his expression 'wild explosion,' as this offers an interesting concept considering all the things I have written. We could say the T-word has wildly escaped the realms of all conformists and is now in the hands of the nonconformist, but this is just a play on words. Taking any person's life is wrong, and the people who portray themselves as leaders of these radical groups don't possess any special right to dispense life. I would say they are different and may need help, as I'm sure their capacity for kindness is not lost. They can be kind and loving as all humans can, but maybe they are misguided through years of conditioning or brainwashing.

I ask now that all gullible people seeking to be recognised stand up. I could have used such words as downtrodden or oppressed, but the meaning of 'gullible' is 'easily fooled or cheated; especially: quick to believe something that is not true.' Being downtrodden or oppressed, to me, means living without hope due to being treated badly by powerful people or groups. So I use word 'gullible' here in the broadest sense, as we know there are these people out there. But I have never heard anyone stand up and shout, 'We need all you gullible people to join us, as you are gullible!'

I am nearly 100 per cent sure that there would be limited volunteers in this case, as no one would want to be considered gullible. Just think, you are standing in that room and the speakers say, 'We shall only take the gullible ones, so please stand up now.' If anyone did stand up we would all look at the gullible one and think, *poor soul*. However, we are all gullible if we don't think for ourselves. I have heard well-trained talkers say things like, 'Stand up! Protect our beliefs!' Which beliefs are they talking about? I'm never 100 per cent sure. I may be wrong, but I cannot remember any of the great prophets promoting murder and the taking of innocent lives. I have only read of miracles, kindness, and love.

As I am not a prophet or one of greatness, I can say to any person or government that promotes or allows atrocities against others, 'You don't deserve to share the same oxygen as the majority of people that truly want to live in peace!'

I must be careful here, as I am considering the leaders and others who carry out these crimes against humankind as mentally sane. Maybe that's the issue; the world is reacting, instead of being proactive. Maybe instead of spending trillions of dollars on defence and weaponry, we need to create a preventative funding system that funds communities to reduce radicalism. Maybe we could start by honestly looking at the mental health of the world's population.

One person in the world dies by suicide every 40 seconds, according to the first ever comprehensive report on the issue from the World Health Organisation, which talks of a massive toll of tragic and preventable deaths.

Suicide rates vary enormously from one country to another around the world – influenced by the cultural, social, religious and economic environments in which people live and sometimes want to stop living. Some of the worst affected countries have more than 40 times more suicides than the least affected areas. But the pressures that cause extreme emotional distress are similar everywhere and there are measures all governments can take to make suicide less likely, says the WHO.

—*The Guardian* **newspaper, 4 September 2014**

This article intrigued me. In my own country, Australia, a talk show aired in April 2015 reported that each day, seven people take their own lives in Australia and as many as 1 million do so worldwide. And for every person that succeeds, another twenty people will try and not succeed, going on to live with the physical and mental scars.

What does this have to do with terrorism or other individuals that kill others? I think it has a lot to do with terrorism, as I honestly don't think a person of sound mind could believe that torturing and taking another's life is sane. I would like to ask a question: Which holy book promotes suicide?

I may be wrong, but I don't think any of the established religions do. In fact, several religions consider it a sin. Some countries consider it a crime, which is a little harsh, as mental illness needs to be understood and treated, not considered a sin or a crime. What is a sin and a crime, is promoting harm to another due to perceived differences.

While nothing is easier to denounce the evildoer, nothing is more difficult than to understand him.

—Fyodor Dostoevsky

Considering the quotation above, I shall say here that people are people, and people are scared of the unknown. Quite often, they refuse to listen to or accept anything that is against their beliefs. How shallow this makes the average person! However, before I continue to imply all terrorists are mindless madmen who need medical care, one needs to explore more. People who commit suicide, in general, experience hopelessness and depression. I'm sure suicide bombers, though, see their actions as works of heroism and honour.

So what is the difference in basic terms? In my humble opinion, a person who commits suicide due to hopelessness and depression is looking for escape, as they feel their life is worthless and it would be better for their friends and family if they were no longer around.

However, this decision, in the majority of cases, is made alone without instructions or conditioning by others. I always think it is a cry for help that is never heard and one that can never be answered.

However, a suicide bomber could believe God has sent him on a mission. Many believe, according to the books and articles written on the subject, that they are motivated by belief in a better and happier afterlife. Some may believe they shall receive heavenly rewards. We must also consider those that are struggling to survive and want a better life for their families. They see limited opportunities for advancement. Then one day they are told that if they strap a bomb onto themselves and willingly take their lives and the lives of others, their families shall be looked after and they need never worry. Their motivation now is twofold. These people are not gullible nor mentally ill. They are humans who have lost their way and need help.

Therefore suicide bombers do not see taking their lives as suicide. Instead, they may see it as an act of sacrifice and even kindness. With all the horror and violence that may surround them, they do not even consider the innocent people that they shall kill. They may think, 'If I do not do this, someone else will, and their families will be looked after and mine shall suffer.' However, this is John just exploring the 'why' question and trying to make sense of senseless killing. But the why shall remain unanswered, as only the person who commits suicide or becomes a suicide bomber can really answer it.

Not to confuse things, I don't think a child or adult wakes up one day and says, 'I want to become a suicide bomber.' I just cannot accept this is a thought that comes into a twelve-year old's mind. It must be conditioned. Many individuals, in my view, are being indoctrinated at an early age or after traumatic instances where they have lost family and friends or they see limited hope for themselves and their families. This is where they receive comfort through spiritual learning or false hope and promises. The radical preachers may place a great spiritual importance on purifying the world and sacrificing their lives or taking the lives of others, whereby their sins shall be forgiven as this is a holy war.

Hello! History repeating itself! Sadly, I must say here that nothing really changes. During the first Christian crusades that occurred in 1095, which were promoted and encouraged by Pope Urban II, the masses were told that if they went and fought, they would be forgiven for all their past sins and be guaranteed a place in heaven. What misguided fools they were and still are.

Any religious group promoting brutality, torture, and outright terrorism against other human beings is wrong. I shall say this openly, as this in my opinion is against the Almighty and the God of your religion. But still we hear the same thing over and over again. The people in power mislead people to act while being told they will be honoured and considered martyrs under the eyes of our lord. I'm sorry, but I don't believe this. I repeat, any religious leader past, present, or future who says this is wrong. And those who follow these misguided instructions and radical beliefs are also wrong. This is my perception and not the perception of the thousands of followers of radical groups across the world.

Terrorists tend to have an apocalyptic worldview and to see the world as precariously balanced between good and evil. They believe that through their actions, they can uphold their values of family, religion, ethnicity, and nationality and bring about the triumph of the good. Acting on God's behalf to defend these values is viewed as more important than life.

—Michelle Maiese

I love the concept of good versus evil. Am I being good or evil as I write this chapter on terrorism? I'm sure we all struggle with the concept of what is evil. I think you may already understand my view of evil, but it could be different from yours, especially if we play on words and use the word 'sinful'. This word is quite often used to gain support within religious groups. It may be just a word, but it is a powerful word that can drive some to commit crimes against humanity, thinking their acts will clean the world of sinners. I was once told by an Irish priest that there are more sinners inside the church than outside the church. I do not know if this is a fact or if he was just trying to make conversation and make me laugh.

Words are so much more powerful than sticks, stones, and other ways to inflict physical pain and suffering, all because of differences of opinion, beliefs, culture, and values. I would agree and disagree, in part, with Maiese's article, as it reports that terrorists tend to have an apocalyptic world view. I think this is a human's general view, when you consider what we do to our planet in the name of advancements. I would also say here that I don't condone attacks or the taking of another person's country due to opposing beliefs. What I do condone is forgiveness. I would like to see a world in which we help each other to heal the wrongs of the past and advance into the future. Only then may we humans be allowed to transcend into the next life.

In this life, we have to make many choices. Some are very important choices. Some are not. Many of our choices are between good and evil. The choices we make, however, determine to a large extent our happiness or our unhappiness, because we have to live with the consequences of our choices.

—James E. Faust

If I were to play the devil's advocate and look for a common denominator between terrorism and increased domestic worldwide suicide, I could argue that the key is sociality and the widening gap between those who have and those who do not have. Embarrassment, poverty, and hopelessness often give rise to a sense of outrage and desperation, which can lead to depression, suicide, anger, and feelings of being wronged. This sounds like the perfect ingredients for an extremist leader looking for recruits. For people with nothing to lose, desperation and martyrdom provide the ultimate escapes from life's predicaments.

According to Jessica Stern in *Terror in the Name of God*, terrorists are often individuals who feel deeply humiliated and confused about their future path, or are frustrated about the political climate in which they live. Nevertheless, this does not explain why well-educated and middle-class people enrol in terrorist movements – or maybe it does. These people will become angry when they are typecast through the media as having certain qualities due to their religion, culture, and values, which, as I said, is totally unfair and misleading. However, this is occurring. Humans are humans, and we all get angry and frustrated when we feel insulted or perceive that our beliefs are not being accepted or respected. We act, and sometimes, I'm sure, we act on emotion and not reason.

I am not suggesting or offering excuses for those who do turn to violence, nor would I ever agree that any group or government has the right to terrorise any individual or group. What I am saying is, we need to truly understand why people turn into terrorists and look at how we can prevent this before it occurs. I promoted before a prevention fund, one that is spent on healing and treating people and not on defence or buying more weapons to kill and maim people.

Sorry, lightbulb moment! I have just had another thought on why terrorism and suicide across the world are increasing. Here, I would like to imply that globalisation is the major cause of both terrorism and increased rates of suicides, as countries export all their wares without consideration of others' cultures, beliefs, or values. The receivers' governments open their doors to create trade, believing this will bring a better life for their people, without realising the rich and powerful will get richer and more powerful while breaking the backs of the poor by making them more and more reliant and needy. In turn, this influences and drives changes in culture, beliefs, and values, and in some instances, it can cause conflicts and torments between the old and young. The old see values and customs being forgotten while the young may not understand why they need to maintain values and customs that they do not believe in. Their generation lives in a totally different environment, where more things are available and more is wanted. They do not consider the life they live now is due to the sacrifices and hard word of generations gone by. However, we should not blame our young. I'm sure all past generations would say they did what they did to ensure future generations would have a better life.

A passing thought: even with all the terrorist acts and violence across the world, this century is still currently considered the most peaceful one ever. The world is not falling apart, never mind the headlines, where we are continually exposed to doom and gloom. There are good things happening, and in general, we humans do try and look after each other. I would even say the majority of people on this Earth are more responsive and willing to help each other now than in the past.

My shoe size, is size 11, and all people with my shoe size could wear my shoes, but they may not be able to walk the same path that I have chosen.

—JRC, 'Mr John'

To close, I shall say: Don't panic. Most of us shall be killed or die by some boring, mundane thing. Life is good, so live it with an open mind and accepting heart.

CHAPTER 18

What Does a Man Need to Be, to Be a Man?

Men are like steel. When they lose their temper, they lose their worth.

—Chuck Norris

I've called this chapter 'What Does a Man Need to Be, to Be a Man?' as I'm a little confused. I thought the world was changing and equality was understood. Now, I didn't say equality was being implemented, but I thought that at least the majority of people knew about it. So I'm surprised when I still hear young boys say, 'Men need to be tough, strong, and never show weaknesses, 'Men shouldn't cry', or 'Men must work to provide for the family'. However, this last statement is something that I do believe in. If you decide to take on the role of a husband and father, you should also take on the responsibility of providing for those that you love. I am not trying to make any man out there feel inadequate, but you should be held accountable for when you do not provide.

Men, and I mean all men, need to stop being stereotyped. For a start, I am John R Christian, and though I am a man, I am my own man. I am neither the man my father used to be nor am I the man next door (unless I live next door to you). I understand who and what I am. I am a man.

We Homo Sapiens have evolved, and our predecessors the Neanderthals have been extinct for over 30,000 years, give or take a year, month, or day. Now, I'm sure some of you may argue that we're not all that evolved, especially when you see how some men act. I have watched many a man sulk and complain, witnessed others become too loud after a few drinks, and heard of others wanting to be mothered and nursed when they are a little sick. Ah, and I could be speaking about myself. However, in my defence and the defence of others, recent studies have found that the majority of the population have a little Neanderthal within their gene pool, so let's blame our ancestors for our bad behaviour. I mean, we always have to blame someone or something, as we are men! Come on, let's be honest: We like to blame others, don't we? I find people who blame others for something they did or could not do shallow.

So, allow me to consider what a man has to do, or portray, in order to be considered a man. Do we need to be strong? Do we need to be able to fight? Do we need to be fearless? Do we need to hunt, kill, and treat women as possessions? In my opinion it is OK for men to cry, show emotions, cook, iron, and stay at home to look after the children. However, this is my opinion. In some countries, and not just Asian countries, men who stay at home (because his wife is able to earn more, or for other reasons) are frowned upon. Well, not in my world. Do what works for you and your family, as this is part of being a modern-day man. So we come back to the same question: What *is* a man, anyway?

I must be very careful here, as a great author has already written a book entitled *What is Man*. I wonder if you know who I'm talking about. If I were to say Samuel Langhorne Clemens (1835–1910), would that ring any bells for you? Or should I just say Mark Twain? I'm sure you're more familiar with the latter, but that was Mr Clemens' pen name. I wonder, when someone writes under a pen name, do they feel more freedom to explore and express ideas? Is it because they can see the world not through their own eyes but through the eyes of an imaginary person? I shall write a book on why famous and not-so-famous people need to change their names or create alter egos. However, before that book is written, please feel free to send me your opinions on the subject, as I would very much like to include them in my future book. You can send your opinions and comments to my blog: jchristianblog.wordpress.com

---

Humour is the great thing, the saving thing. The minute it crops up, all our irritations and resentments slip away and a sunny spirit takes their place.

***

In the Spring, I have counted 136 different kinds of weather inside of 24 hours.

***

Each man must for himself alone decide what is right and what is wrong, which course is patriotic and which isn't. You cannot shirk this and be a man. To decide against your conviction is to be an unqualified and excusable traitor, both to yourself and to your country, let men label you as they may.

—Mark Twain

Are we men labelled by other men? Or are we born to be the man we turn into? If that's the case, why should we worry and stress ourselves out? Our destinies are already written by the universe and our parents' gene pool. Therefore, we cannot be blamed for our behaviour, as it is not ours to own.

As I am writing this, I'm listening to the rattling of my air-conditioning system. It seems to be in time with the music I'm playing, which is 'Uluru' by Tony O'Conner. As I listen to this harmony, I think of the many men who are troubled and confused, who are trying to be someone they're not or be what they don't want to be. In the past,

I had a reputation for being able to fight. And I must admit here, I have had several fights. Most were started by others, but some were started by my own foolishness and need to be accepted. But this was not the person I wanted to be, as I do not like fighting. We all see the world as it appears to us. Some will see all that surrounds them, but others will see the world from within. Meanwhile, there are those who will see it from where they stand. Wherever you see the world, please see it as it is. This is your world, though I'm sad to say, it's also 'a man's world'.

Now, I'm not being sexist or gender intolerant here. I'm telling it as I see, through a man's eyes. Governments and companies may talk about equality, but do you really think half the population (an estimated 3.5 billion women) are treated equally? I would say no, because it's still very much a man's world. The world is being run by men, and if you think I'm wrong, just look at our governments. Consider this: How many women hold seats in those governments, and how many hold the power of government?

For those men who believe that all should be treated equally and that equality is right for all, I shall say, Great! But please remember this: Put your thoughts into actions! Words alone won't change the ruling elite or the masses. You may not be in a position to change the mind-set of millions, as you're not in control of millions, but you are in control of your own mind and your own actions. Forget what I wrote before that you cannot be blamed for your behaviour. Even though I said you may have a few Neanderthal cells roaming throughout your blood stream, you still need to be your best. You can and will. So take control! Show the best of you, the person that is within all of us. Always think of the people who love us for who we are. Look at the person who loves you and appreciate that love. Never belittle them or their respect for you. If you do, you are belittling yourself. Make this world a beautiful world, a world where all are safe, respected, and free.

I think a person with dignity is a person who is easily liked, a person of honour who will show others respect. They will have strong principles without being shallow or bloody-minded, and they will have a sense of pride in themselves.

This will reflect how they carry themselves and act, as they will respect themselves for what they are. And more importantly, in most cases, they will like the person they are. This makes it easier for them to respect and like others. What a simple philosophy. Do you like the person you are?

Lock me away, take my clothes, my food and all those materialistic things that I may think are important, but please leave me my dignity.

—JRC

I shall say here that I'm sure there isn't a perfect man or a perfect woman. There are good people whom others look up to and try to emulate. But I think, instead of trying to imitate another person, one should get to know the person who is standing in front of the mirror, as this is the person whom others see. As I said before, I am John R Christian. When I look into the mirror, I see a person who has lived, suffered, and caused pain to others. But I also see what others now see, and it is who I am. I no longer portray anything else than what I am. I am content with this and, more importantly, do not need to put on any alter egos or hide behind anyone or anything.

CHAPTER 19

Animals

People are not going to care about animal conservation unless they think that animals are worthwhile.

—David Attenborough

Angry moments rarely come my way, as I work hard to never get angry. But the readers of this chapter may begin to think that I'm quite cranky, which I assure you, I'm not. I'm just being opinionated and saying what I feel: that we humans need to wake up and consider what we are doing to this planet and all the creatures that live here with us.

Will man destroy all the wonders of this Earth with our greed and exploding populations? Now, in the twenty-first century, we continue to need more land and resources for our selfish developments. We do not consider the harm we are inflicting, whereby we destroy the most beautiful and pristine natural environments and the habitats of others species.

Our selfish 'me me' attitude makes us forget that we stole this land from kinder creatures that only live to survive and reproduce. But we don't recognise this. All we know and say is they are 'native animals,' meaning animals that roamed these lands and were not introduced by man. I use the word 'native' as I do not like the word 'wild'. As compared to man, they are not 'wild,' they are natural and native to the land. However, for those of you who consider these animals wild, that is your choice. I agree that we humans have classified many things, but I say 'native' instead of classifying them as wild animals, as I do not think they are wild. Let's consider them as living creatures that now have to survive in the face of even greater threats. It's all due to us humans destroying their habitats. Therefore, I see them as less wild than man. Man kills for fun; animals kill to survive. And why does man consider any animal to be wild? Is it because anything that we haven't captured, imprisoned, and then domesticated is wild to our eyes.

Heaven forbid that we should live harmoniously with undomesticated animals. It would never work! We kick up a fuss and call the local authorities as soon as an undomesticated creature comes close. We demand that the animal be destroyed, as it a pest that came into our yard, garden, or city to scavenge for food and pull rubbish from our bins. We say, 'This is our home! This is our land!' But we are wrong. We are the intruders, not them. We have stolen their land and homes and removed what was once their habitat, a natural and beautiful place. Now we offer them in return our concrete malls, higher-than-high tower blocks, and unimaginable housing estates. If we're lucky, we'll have a small garden, where we plant non-native plants to make us think we are doing the right thing and going green.

We are so lazy we even buy artificial plants to decorate our homes that need no care or attention. Oh, Mr Population, please wake up! These are the things that are killing our planet and our minds. We need nature, not plastic plants!

We are connected to this Earth. Our feet need to feel the earth beneath them. We need to feel the ocean breaking across our bodies, and we need to walk through open fields and natural forests. We need to look at all that grows in awe as we lose ourselves in the richness of colours and the natural architecture that nature gives us. All this is free if we stop destroying it. Otherwise it will cost us lots, and not just in monetary terms.

Or should I say, all of this was free until we started to live our ever-wanting lives of 'give me more' without any consideration for the harm we were doing and still do, all under the name of progress. How can this be advancement, when we are killing nature and turning once beautiful and fertile landscapes into barren dust bowls that cannot support the lives of the creatures that once called it home? We should stop turning our backs or closing our eyes to the damage that we have done and consider the people of the future whom we may never meet or know. They will grow up never knowing what it was like in times gone by, as all they have now is their concrete jungle with their artificial gardens, documentaries, and stories of what the earth was like before their ancestors stripped it bare.

The bicycle is a former child's toy that has now been elevated to icon status because, presumably, it can move the human form from pillar to post without damage to the environment.

—Brock Yates

The bicycle that once was every child's dream has now become an environmental solution to reducing our population's carbon footprint. I know environmentalists want us to do more than build bicycle lanes and promote bike riding to reduce our carbon footprints, but please let's understand. Future generations of children will be told about how the seas were once blue and crystal clear, full of edible, healthy fish. They will learn that our skies were once blue and we could breathe the air without fear of clogging our lungs with filth and manmade toxic chemicals that we continually released into the atmosphere, or that we could hear the call of nature through the songs of millions of birds that no longer live, as they have nowhere to live.

Stories, films, and documentaries cannot replace all that is lost. Future generations will not be able to explain with clarity the beauty of what was once real and taken from this land. How can we explain the feeling of cleaner-than-clean air that was free for all to breathe without any need of purification systems? How can we explain the beauty of walking through million-year-old forests and the smell of nature in it richest form? Or how we never dreaded getting wet, as rainfall was welcomed to water our crops and even to refresh our bodies without fear of it being polluted or acidified?

How can we explain all that has been taken without crying and feeling guilt for what will never return? Those people will never know the sensation of what was taken. So how will the future generations be able to close their eyes and allow their imaginations to explore? Will they be able to tell their children what has been lost? The answer here is possibly no, and it is no longer important. Their experience will be one of being fed man-made chemicals, and they will live without understanding what it's like to shop and buy fresh fruit and vegetables, meat, poultry, and fish. They will not understand the pleasure in preparing dinner so you can sit with your family and friends and eat. They may feel all this was a waste, as they can now receive all their nourishment from a single capsule. They live in ignorant bliss, locked away from the decimated world that has lost the will to live due to mankind's unwillingness to listen to the cries of nature, all because we believed that we had the power to fix what we knowingly destroyed. However, we cannot blame those people whom we shall never meet, as it is us who are causing the damage due to our greed and insatiable needs to feed and entertain the ever-growing population of the world.

If we're destroying our trees and destroying our environment and hurting animals and hurting one another and all that stuff, there's got to be a very powerful energy to fight that. I think we need more love in the world. We need more kindness, more compassion, more joy, more laughter. I definitely want to contribute to that.

—Ellen DeGeneres

The year is 2015, and as I write this, I think of how I have witnessed a bird build a nest in absolute amazement. I sat for hours just watching it fly away, looking for that right piece of stick, leaf, or natural product to build a home with. He hopes his design shall please his mate and in it they can raise their family together, However, as I watch, I realise this is not an easy task. He will build and rebuild it until his mate is content. And if this work of art is not correctly done, she will fly away to find another mate that has the skills and ability to build her a nest of her liking.

With their natural habitat slowly being taken away, birds now build nests from man-made products polluting what was once a piece of nature built solely with natural products. Now they struggle in an environment that is continually changing, selecting man-made products and entwining them into the work of art. Why? Well, I'm sure it is not for beauty or to give the nest a plastic bag feel. It is because we are destroying their native habitat. We are destroying our habitat, as the forests, oceans, and all that live on this planet are ours to enjoy. We shall never own it, and I honestly feel we shall never truly appreciate it. We humans are always looking not at what we have but what we may have. However, when it comes to our planet, we don't have the vision to understand the damage and our inability to give back what we have taken.

If only I had a magic wand, like in a Disney epic or fairy tale. I could then conjure up a mystical spell. Then we could understand all animals and all living things are meant to live and we humans should have courage and kindness, as Cinderella was told by her mother. And maybe we would then stop playing God and realise we are all just apprentices learning our trades. Then fear appears in my mind, as I think of wicked witches or evil sorcerers. If they had the magic wand, would they use it for good, to fix the damage that has been done, or to create fear and more damage? Therefore, I have changed my mind. No wishing for a mystical spell or magic wand!

I wish, instead, that we humans would have a lightbulb moment, where we start to see and respond by understanding that even the smartest person is still learning. So please, learn that the Earth needs our love and kindness. It will offer us its magic by rejuvenating and growing once again, so animals can roam and birds will again have the natural materials to build their nests without having to look for substitutes.

I wonder if my words have made you at least think. Maybe I could ask you to close your eyes and imagine being a bird, spider, snake, or any animal that you like. Can you imagine how they feel? And please, don't put your logical hat on. Tell me these living things don't feel as we do. Maybe that is the problem. We don't see and feel as they do.

Humans are amphibians – half spirit and half animal. As spirits they belong to the eternal world, but as animals they inhabit time.

—**C. S. Lewis**

I closed my eyes, and I felt the wings of a bird stretching from the centre of my back. They were heavy and untrained. I clenched my fist, and as I did, I imagined my wings moving. I made my fingers move and felt the feathers flutter. I opened my arms, and my wings stretched beyond the length of my arms. I moved my arms up and down and felt my wings take flight. Now I was flying, looking down at the world from above. I saw as a bird would see. I glided across the sky, where every now and then I would swoop, dive, and allow the turbulent air to take me higher. I was weightless. I feel this was freedom, but maybe the bird looks at us and thinks, *If I could only be a human, I would be strong and would have no need to fly.*

Who knows what they feel? But we could at least try and understand that it is not natural to tame and cage animals. This is unnatural, just as it is unnatural for humans to be imprisoned against their will or not allowed to speak, love, or be the person they were born to be.

I have said several times that I'm like Peter Pan. I can relate to being a man who has never forgotten how to be a boy, so I can laugh and cry without feeling ashamed. These are natural emotions that we should never lock away, nor should we lock away any other emotion, especially those that give us the strength and courage to stand up for what is right. We should protect this earth so those whom we shall never know can enjoy nature by being a part of it, so their senses can come alive while walking and seeing, hearing, touching, smelling, and tasting all that can be experienced in real time. If we succeed, there will be no need to imagine what may have been. Then we will not have to say, 'Look at the wonders we've invented to save you time and to offer you pleasure, so you don't have to leave your concrete jungles, where you breathe purified air, eat your man-made, chemically enhanced food supplements, and wonder, "What if our ancestors had done what was right?"'

I like nonsense, it wakes up the brain cells. Fantasy is a necessary ingredient in living, it's a way of looking at life through the wrong end of a telescope. Which is what I do, and that enables you to laugh at life's realities.

—Dr Seuss

I started this chapter by saying that angry moments are rare for me, and I shall finish by not apologising if my words came across as more abrupt and harsh than usual. I think people need to own up and stop blaming others for not doing enough. To save this planet, we need to consider what we can do and do it.

Use the power of your vote to elect greener governments. Consider the small things, and never think that we cannot make a difference. We can, but we need to start now and not wait.

Don't think that some brighter person shall come up with a mystical spell or magical fix. You have the magic within you. With the actions you take today, you have the ability to help our environment. You can protect our native animals. You can leave a living legacy to people you will never meet, a hundred years from now.

CHAPTER 20

Are We in Control?

We do not choose nonexistence; nor do we choose complete awareness. We slog on, in a kind of foggy cognitive middle land we call sane, a place where we almost never acknowledge the haze.

—Martha Stout

I've just had another lightbulb moment! After reading years of news and listening to governments across world and the never-ending babble of politicians, I just realised that I totally misunderstood all that was written and said. But then again, the majority of the articles written and political speeches given weren't about giving a clear and accurate picture of events or driving change that would be beneficial to the masses. They were about being popular. They were never actually about reports that were factual, true, or even possible. They had to be popular. Lies and more lies, one may say. But in their defence, I'm sure they like to believe that they can achieve something; even if that something is a mystical tale with a not-so-happy ending.

However, the majority of the theatrical stories tellers shall survive while the masses continually tread water trying to keep afloat, thinking change must occur. This person who wears a nicely tailored suit and speaks with such confidence must not be trying to fool us. Oh joy! I can now smile and say *fuck,* as the world population is having lightbulb moments and rebelling with the aim of establishing a better life for themselves and future generations. I believe the majority of the world is just surviving, living day to day. When will the world powers and those unscrupulous politicians repent and do the right thing? Sigmund Freud may have called it an 'everyday misery', or he may have related it to some overwhelming need to be loved. I shall let you explore Freud's theories and just offer my opinions.

In chapter 17, I discussed suicide and many other points that may drive someone to become a terrorist. But I did not totally explore the ultimate choice, where individuals decide whether to live or die. Please don't close the book just yet! I promise I won't take this chapter into soul-searching, mind-blasting doom and gloom. Instead, I will take it to a place so you may think, *Ahh.* Take a deep breath.

I shall start it with a question:

Do you think the majority of the world's population is truly living a good life? Or are they just surviving from day to day?

I am never sure if any of my readers complete the questions I give them. Therefore, I always feel the need to answer them myself. If anything, it's to offer my opinion and not leave it open. My answer to above question is: *I feel the majority of the world is just surviving and doing what is needed to live, as they have chosen to live.*

I shall pray that all people, from all religious groups, genders, and nationalities, will have a great life where they can laugh, love, and enjoy. I feel it's important to live your life and hope that we can all be exposed to a life that is truly a wonderful experience. I believe it needs to be vibrant, filled with passion, love, and a little silliness. I didn't say you had to be rich to achieve this, as you do not. Therefore, let's not demonise or rationalise humans. Let's just accept that we are all different, and I would say 80 to 90 per cent of us would be extremely happy and content surviving, as surviving is important to humans.

Maybe this is why the majority like to believe the views of a political party, which claims to represent the common people. Oh! This makes me laugh! I'm not sure it is politically correct to class any particular group as 'the common people.' That sounds rude, judgemental, and class discriminatory to me. Or maybe I am just over-analysing it. That wouldn't do, as I said I don't want this chapter to be soul-searching. However, I did look up the term 'common people' on Wikipedia.

The terms common people, commoners, or the masses denote a broad social division referring to ordinary people who are members of neither the nobility nor the priesthood.

—Wikipedia

Now I am laughing out loud. I have never met an 'ordinary' person in my life, as we are all different. I have met some very ordinary politicians, leaders, and priests, but maybe the world is changing. Maybe the ordinary is now the minority, not the majority.

It is the minority that is ruling the world, not the majority. But I'm not sure if this minority is truly living. Rich or poor, I would say here, each and every moment can be a struggle for all of us, and it doesn't matter which group you belong to.

Each morning, we all start the same: by opening our eyes, as we have chosen to live and not die. My friend and editor, Adline, says she likes this statement but then asks me to explain it more. I cannot write an explanation for all, but I can write one for me. I choose to live because I will not be alive forever. So why not live and do my best to enjoy what I have? These years we are given on Earth should be considered as precious. Therefore, I shall plod on, doing what I must do to survive. And as I have written before, I believe life is about identifying opportunities and then making a choice. This is easy to write, but making a choice can be quite hard. The majority of people like routines, so when we are offered an opportunity that requires us to make a decision, quite often we have to step outside our surviving zones. This zone is where we place ourselves so we wake up and do those things we may not like to do. But we do them to survive, and quite often, this takes us out of our comfort zones, where we can relax and never feel pressured or stressed. A comfort zone for most is when everything is going as planned and you feel in control. The surviving zone is the zone that we step into to make money to put food on the table, roof over our heads and when we are in this zone things may not go as we thought or planned. However, sometimes our survival zones becomes our comfort zone as we are no longer dream or have the will to look for change.

If we choose not to step outside our comfort zones and never accept challenges by stepping outside our survival zones, later in life we may consider what it would have been like and may even say 'if only.' We self-analyse, and moreover, we ask the question, 'What if?' We get confused and sometimes scared, offering reasons why we should not accept this new opportunity. We surmise, this could make our lives harder than just plodding on and surviving. Tick, tick, tick. The clock is ticking, and time is going by, so let's just stay within our survival zones, which allow us to be able to drift into our comfort zones. Let's just accept our mundane lives. But – and as I always say, there is always a *but* – if you are unhappy look at the simple things that could make you happy. Years ago when my children were young, we had little money, and we were surviving week to week. But we still found the time to go out and walk alone on the beach or run in the fields and make up silly stories. I have been accused of being a dreamer, but these dreams gave me hope. From hope I start to see opportunities and believe I could do more than just survive. Now as I look back I am pleased that I stepped outside my surviving zone and moved beyond that comfort zone to the zone that I am in today, a zone that allows me to work, write, and play but still walk along a beach, run through the field, and make up silly stories to make my friends' children laugh. So stop complaining and make the best of the choices you have made, understanding each year you live is a precious one.

Once you can do this, you will feel a new zest in your life, as you will find contentment and happiness. These two very important elements come from within. Therefore, they are always with us, waiting to be discovered and then unwrapped.

Are you ready to unwrap these special elements and accept your life as it is? Or do you want to explore more and take one of those opportunities that will arrive? As I said, this will require you to make changes in your life. It may expose you to new challenges, where your stress levels may rise until you get used to whatever you have chosen to do. And this then becomes your new comfort zone.

However, I would be amiss if I didn't advise you to be careful. The grass on the other side is not always greener and still needs to be fertilised and mowed. It may even be fake! Let's be honest, no one likes a copy or fake product. So strive, step up, step out, and go for what makes you happy.

I am content sitting alone. I am content being in a crowd. I am content … These are the most beautiful words. And even better, being content makes me happy.

CHAPTER 21

Nowhere

Imagination will often carry us to worlds that never were. But without it we go nowhere.

—Carl Sagan

Over the previous twenty chapters, we have explored many of my opinions and views covering silly, meaningful, and in some cases provocative thoughts. This is all with the aim of making you, the reader, think and explore your own feelings and emotional attachment to an idea, thought, or opinion.

This is my third book. My first, *Bring Me a Higher Life,* was published as a paperback, while my second, *Table for Two, Sex Not Included,* was an e-book. My second to me also marked a separation from my publisher, True Wealth, but not from my loyal and wonderful friend and editor, Adline. So as I write what I consider to be the last chapter of my third book, I can't help but wonder if it will be published or forever sit idle within a hard drive full of thoughts, opinions, and silliness.

If you are reading this, some mythical, wand-carrying house elf has granted me another dream, where I can share my views and opinions. Hopefully you will enjoy my ranting. "As I am reading this

212

now, the last statements seems silly as I am reading if for the final time before being published oh thank you, oh mythical publishing wizard".

Ranting is good, isn't it? I will not answer this, nor should you, unless you need to rant. Then please, just do it. 'But why rant?' I hear my inner voice say. Because It allows you to express a feeling, be it nice, bad, or indifferent. It blows the cobwebs off of your soul. It blows off inner steam and reduces pressure and even stress. But please be mindful about who you are ranting to. My best rants are to myself, when I run, swim, or drive.

This chapter is titled 'Nowhere,' but before I explore this, let's consider what chapter 13 was about. In that chapter, I argued against the idea of people putting themselves forward as nobody or, worse, someone putting another human down by saying they are nobody. Why would I mention this? Because I can and I want to. Plus, this chapter is about another nowhere, where I am sure we may find lots of discarded nobodies.

This chapter, being the last one, will finish with a smile and laugh, as usual in John's World, which can be considered nowhere. But as always, it is still somewhere, as I allow my imagination to untie all things captured within my life while trying to create pages of words that are meaningful, while being light-hearted and meaningless.

Let's dream of a wonderful holiday. Close your eyes, and allow your thoughts to offer you pictures of the most serene and peaceful place, where you can rest and rejuvenate your batteries of life. Or maybe you need excitement and an extreme sport to take you away from your everyday life.

One person's concept of the perfect holiday may be another's person nightmare. For example, my idea of camping is booking into a nice hotel in the country, sliding the windows open, and drinking coffee on a balcony while breathing in fresh air and looking at the beauty that surrounds me. Meanwhile, others may enjoy lying on the hard ground covered only by thinner than thin fabric, being eaten by little insects that don't like people who've laid fabric on their homes.

Still, those happy campers shall say, sleepless nights and getting eaten alive by insects are wonderful!

However, if I were to generalise, I would say most holidays seem like hard work, with the planning, the doing, the sightseeing, and the meeting and greeting of relatives and others when all you really wanted to do was escape. Is this why when someone is asked how their holiday was, I've heard them say more than once, 'I am glad to be back at work for a rest'? That always makes me smile, as I thought work was a place to work, not rest. Whoops! Now I have my meaner-than-mean manager's hat on, where I expect production and efficiency.

However, I like holidays and often ask my wife where she would like to go to next. What if I said to her, and you, that on your next holiday, I want to take you to nowhere? I can hear some readers saying, 'What now? I never go anywhere.' Well, I'm sure you will not think this. Sorry, I escaped to John's World for a moment, where I imagined this wonderful place, Nowhere, where I am allowed to escape being at work or being at home or surrounded by people. Is there such a place? Dorothy clicked her red shoes and travelled the yellow brick road, and Peter lived forever in Neverland.

I do not have any red shoes, and I am not sure if Tinkerbell will sprinkle fairy dust to help me find my way. If I went to the travel agent and asked for a brochure on Nowhere, they might call for someone to take me away.

We are dealing with the best-educated generation in history. But they've got a brain dressed up with nowhere to go.

—Timothy Leary

I thought this quotation by Timothy Leary very suitable, as advancements within technology, science, and all things that go ping do not allow the majority to use their imagination freely. We have become a population expecting someone will know, and better still, we can find answers by doing an Internet search, as everything is within a stroke of a keyboard.

This isn't just happening among the young. A while ago I was having coffee, a great pastime of mine, and watching people. I watched two elderly people discussing something. In the middle of the conversation, one went to her phone and totally ignored the other as he carried on talking. Then, with a smile, she said, 'Look. This is the answer, and you are wrong.' Google, I would imagine, solved another argument – or created one, But that made me smile. How many arguments are settled or created due to instant searches or Internet browsing?

Maybe she was searching for nowhere. So where is nowhere, and why would I like you to visit there? Nowhere, to me, is a place where I can sit and unwind. Where I refuse to look at my phone or reply to text or e-mails. Where I take time to rest and be still. Where I can climb into my world while being within an arm's reach of your world and within this universe. This place I talk about is your place, a special place where you can lose yourself for thirty minutes. That's right, thirty minutes. *Why thirty?* I hear the inquisitive mind ask. I believe you should take time out for yourself every day, and thirty minutes is what I allow myself. You may want an hour or just thirteen minutes and thirty-three seconds – whatever! How long is not the point. What is required is that we escape and reenergise.

I just had a silly thought. I expect you are an adult reading this book, but what happens when you step outside your adulthood? Don't be worried. All I want you to do is pick up an old classic, such as *Alice's Adventures in Wonderland* or *Alice through the Looking Glass*. Or if these are not adventurous enough, what about *Gulliver's Travels, The Jungle Book,* or Moby Dick?

You may think I'm digressing, as these are children's storybooks, and what has this got to do with nowhere? It has everything to do with understanding it is cool to go nowhere. Going nowhere allows you to do things that if you went somewhere, you would be too busy to do. Remember your last holiday? All that running around before you even left? And once there, all that sightseeing and visiting relatives, never having time to just sit and relax? Let's not forget all that money you spent to receive all this extra stress!

So let's de-stress and think of how you can have a holiday every day, whereby you can go nowhere to enjoy yourself. Oh, and it won't cost you any money. A thirty-minute holiday from your day-to-day routine, doing nothing and going nowhere – now that sounds brilliant to me. During my thirty-minute holiday every day, I never push myself to achieve anything, as this is my relaxing time. I can usually be found sitting quietly and reading a book that doesn't need me to analyse anything or read between the lines. The best books for this, I have found, are the old classics, which are pure escapism and quite amusing. I shall not share the one I love most, as I don't want visitors in my nowhere land. Anyway, only you know the book, magazine, or comic that allows you to escape. Now, some may think, *But this could be embarrassing.* I'm not sure why you would think that. This is your time, and what you do in it is up to you.

As I walked home from work the other day, I elected to walk through the park. This, on its own, was relaxing. So while relaxing, I decided to take my thirty-minute holiday and sit on a bench and watch the world go by. I looked around and I could see at least four or five park benches, all vacant. No one was sitting but me. People were busy walking by or talking on their phones, but no one took a break from their day. I sat and opened my bag. I always carry my 'emergency kit' with me of a notebook, pen, and at least two reading books. And normally, one of those books would be an escapism book (my name for a book that I can read without putting my brain into gear). I find fairy tales or the classics can be a great stress release. The book I had with me on this occasion was *The Jungle Book*. So I sat and opened the pages with delight as I read about the adventures of Mowgli the man cub and how he was befriended by a wolf, bears, and Bagheera, the black panther. I shall not ruin the tale. All the animals have names, and the adventure of Mowgli is one that will give you great pleasure and escapism, while not being too far away from your world but still going nowhere.

I also enjoy doing nothing while going nowhere. Sitting still for thirty minutes is a wonderful stress release. But I shall warn you now, this can be challenging for the first few times. We have become a world of fidgets and wrigglers, always wanting to do something. I actually heard the average person's concentration span is less than three minutes!

I am sure I read that Sigmund Freud used to say the average concentration span was between fifteen to twenty minutes. Or did he say every fifteen minutes we think of sex? Now that made you think! What did you think? No need to answer that, as I am sure you are now texting, blogging, or even putting your thoughts on Facebook.

However, back to my point about the concentration span of the average person. After hearing the three-minute claim, I carried out my own experiment by watching people's behaviours. It did not matter where they were and who they were, but my little unprofessional study did concur that people in general find it hard to concentrate on one thing for a long period of time.

Why? we may ask. The reason, I would say, is we are living in a world of gadgets that allow us to be continually connected. We tweet, FaceTime, Facebook, text, e-mail, and Instagram, just to mention a few. All these things have turned us into fidgets and wrigglers.

Now is your time to stop fidgeting and wriggling, unless you have ants in your pants or you are dying to go to the toilet and you are stuck in an elevator. I shall offer you a challenge. Can you and your friends go through a whole dinner without someone checking the phone, answering a text, looking at Facebook, or worse, snapping pictures and posting what you are about to eat, where you are, or other mundane things with the hope you will get a thumbs-up and lots of likes? Are we all so insecure that we need others' approval for what we eat and wear? How many friends does a person need? Or are we becoming a world that needs instant gratification and artificial stimuli, driving us to accept everyone who sends us a friend request? You can chat and gossip with people who are classified as 'friends,' though you may have never met them.

Fidget, wriggle, and let's not concentrate, as I have a friends to like! We are all living in a fidgeting and wriggling world of gadgets that we must continually check, upgrade, and spend more money on. This reduces our ability to concentrate on any one thing for more than a couple of minutes, which is about the same time as an old rock and roll single. Whoops, that was one of those things we older people used to play on a turntable, which was used to listen to music while having great conversations or just hanging out with real people.

All those gadgets and things that we think make our lives better place us under greater pressure. We are missing out on the essential ingredients: communicating with real people in real time, so you can use all your senses to understand what is said and meant. The creative world does not need to develop robots, as large percentages of the human race are being converted into humanised robots! We are conditioned to accept that multimedia devices and social networking are the ultimate platforms to find friends and to communicate. Please wake up and stop sleepwalking throughout your life! Realise there is nothing more wonderful than a conversation with real friends or just sitting silently in the presence of a loved one.

Try to be a rainbow in someone's cloud.

—Maya Angelou

I shall end this chapter by saying I hope you have enjoyed the book and the journey we have travelled together while time has ticked, ticked, ticked by. Please keep enjoying the moments, especially when you take your thirty-minute nowhere holiday to rejuvenate and recharge your life batteries. Life is good.

PS: This little book of self-opinionated bits of drivel was written to express my feelings while trying to make you, the reader, read a book that was written without motive or rhythm. Life is too important to lock yourself away and never allow yourself the time to relax, escape, and explore. My words are written for you. Enjoy, love, and never forget to be nice to each other.

SECOND AND LAST PS:

It is 16 July 2016 just finished my final read and before sending this off and since first putting thought into words nearly three years have passed, no mystical wizard appeared waving their wands ending hatred, greed, jealousy, discrimination, prejudice, bigotry wars, terrorism…Therefore, it up to us the people of the world to open a save the world trust account where each and every one of us deposit kindness, This requires us to be nice, to give, accept, forgive and forget…I hope you enjoy my words and now I end by asking you to tell the person you LOVE, whoever that person is: You love them.

Printed in the United States
By Bookmasters